Anonymous

**Hunt's Philadelphia Guide**

With graphic description of Fairmount park

Anonymous

**Hunt's Philadelphia Guide**
*With graphic description of Fairmount park*

ISBN/EAN: 9783337317546

Printed in Europe, USA, Canada, Australia, Japan

Cover: Foto ©Lupo / pixelio.de

More available books at **www.hansebooks.com**

**1682** | BI-CENTENNIAL EDITION. Revised and Corrected. | **1882**

# HUNT'S
# PHILADELPHIA GUIDE,

With Graphic Description
—OF—
## FAIRMOUNT PARK
—AND—
ALL PLACES AND OBJECTS OF INTEREST.

——ILLUSTRATED.——

Containing New and Complete Alphabetically
**ARRANGED DIRECTORIES OF**

THE STREETS,

THE CHURCHES,

THE CITY RAILWAYS,

AMUSEMENTS, HOTELS, &C., &C.

Given, Name and Number of Street, any House in the City can be accurately located and easily found.

COPYRIGHTED 1882. ALL RIGHTS RESERVED BY

**JOHN P. HUNT,**
PHILADELPHIA.

# PENN MUTUAL LIFE INSURANCE CO.,
### No. 921 Chestnut St., Philadelphia.

ASSETS............$8,000,000 | SURPLUS..........$1,700,000

SAMUEL C. HUEY, President.

**PURELY MUTUAL.** Dividends annually. Policies non-forfeiting for their value. Endowment policies issued at life rates. **Agents wanted.** Apply to **H. S. STEPHENS, Vice-President.**

---

## CONTENTS.

| | |
|---|---|
| Academy of Music............ 40 | Independence Hall............ 30 |
| Academy of Natural Sciences 34 | Insane Asylum................ 38 |
| Amusement Directory........ 58 | Masonic Temple............... 67 |
| Art Gallery................... 57 | Merchants' Exchange ........ 32 |
| Atheneum Buildings.......... 44 | Mercantile Library............ 36 |
| Benevolent Institutions....... 46 | Moyamensing Prison ......... 41 |
| Blind Institute................ 38 | Penn Hospital................. 38 |
| Blockley Almshouse........... 39 | Philadelphia.................... 5 |
| Cemeteries .................... 51 | Philadelphia Library......... 36 |
| Church Directory............. 53 | Post Office.................... 43 |
| City Hall....................... 7 | Public Squares................ 49 |
| City Railway Directory....... 63 | Steam Railroad Directory.... 65 |
| Deaf and Dumb Asylum...... 36 | School of Design for Women 43 |
| Eastern Penitentiary.......... 41 | Street Directory.............. 67 |
| Fairmount Park............... 9 | Telegraph Offices ............. 64 |
| Ferries......................... 65 | U. S. Arsenal................. 38 |
| Friends' Insane Asylum...... 39 | U. S. Custom House.......... 30 |
| Gas Works..................... 44 | U. S. Mint.................... 32 |
| Girard College................ 32 | U. S. Naval Asylum.......... 34 |
| High School................... 44 | University of Pennsylvania... 43 |
| Hotel Directory............... 64 | Water Works.................. 44 |
| House of Refuge.............. 41 | Wills Hospital................. 32 |

Zoological Garden Directory. 60

# PHILADELPHIA.

The City of Brotherly Love embraces now the entire county and contains nearly a million souls (846,980 by the census of 1880;) in manufactures it is pre-eminent among the *cities* of the United States; and, except London, it is believed to be the largest in the world. In the vicinity, and, to some extent, within its limits, water power abounds, and the coal mines within the State yield a convenient and exhaustless supply of fuel for her steam engines. Her laboring population is numerous, skilled and industrious;—these advantages, with that of a large home market, offer inducements to the manufacturer that cannot be found elsewhere. Among the manufactures may be mentioned that of locomotives, whose speed and excellence are celebrated the world over; large numbers of them are exported.

**Forges,** foundries, and almost every species of iron manufacture abound in the suburbs. Sugar refining is a very extensive business in Philadelphia. A large number of hands are employed in lithographing, printing, book binding, etc.; and throughout the business portion of the city, the upper parts of the buildings are thronged with industrious artisans in numberless useful branches of industry.

Philadelphia was planned and settled by William Penn, accompanied by a colony of English Friends or Quakers, in 1682, after a regular purchase from the Indians—ratified by a treaty in due form. The name of Philadelphia (Brotherly Love) was given by William Penn, in part as an embodiment of the principles he intended to carry out in its settlement, and which are a part of the Creed of the Society of Friends, and partly after the ancient city of that name, whose church is spoken of in the book of Revelation. The city rapidly increased, and in three years after the *first* settlement was made, the population was 2500. In 1771 it was incorporated as a city.

The first Congress of the American States was held

THE STATE HOUSE (INDEPENDENCE HALL.)

here Sept. 4, 1774, in Carpenter's Hall (a building still standing), in Carpenter's Court, south from Chestnut, below Fourth. The Convention which formed the Constitution of the United States met in Philadelphia in May, 1787. Here resided the first President of the United States, on Market St. below Sixth, and here Congress assembled for nearly ten years after the adoption of the Constitution. In consequence of the disastrous battles of Germantown and Brandywine, the British had possession of the city from Sept., 1777, to June, 1778. A census taken at this time, by order of Lord Cornwallis, showed the population to be 21,334, exclusive of the army and strangers—the whole of the Whig citizens being also absent. The magnitude and extent of its growth will be understood, when it is stated that on the occasion of the Bi-Centennial Anniversary it contained within its limits (about 130 square miles) over 150,000 dwellings, nearly 15,000 miles of streets, about 400 miles of street car lines, running in every direction and traversing all parts of the city, and about 500 school-houses, built in a substantial manner, the maintenance of which costs nearly two millions a year.

The above is a brief description of the city which Benjamin Franklin, when writing of it, called "Dear, dear, Philadelphia."

## THE NEW CITY HALL.

The architectural design of the new City Hall is essentially modern and presents a rich example of what is known as the *Renaissance*, modified and adapted to the requirements of a great municipality. This immense pile is admirably located on the site of the old Penn Square at Broad and Market. It consists of a single building, occupying an area of 4½ acres, with 525 rooms, probably the largest building on this continent. It is constructed of white marble. The artistic embellishments of decorative stone work, carved in this city from models expressly prepared by home artists, challenges the admiration of all. The grand tower will reach the extraordinary altitude of 535 feet, the highest artificial construction in the world, while at the same time possessing all the elements of strength and firmness.

THE NEW PUBLIC BUILDINGS,
Broad and Market Sts.

# FAIRMOUNT PARK.

The glory of Philadelphia is Fairmount Park. Its situation, its broad expanse, the circumstances of its acquisition, and the peculiar history which is attached to many places within its boundaries, give it an

BRIDGE OVER THE WISSAHICKON AT VALLEY GREEN

unsual interest, not only to the inhabitants of the staid city for whose comfort it has been set apart, but to Americans generally. It lies to the north-west of the great city, and in it, for the streets are reaching out already on both sides of it, and the buildings are crowding against its boundaries. Its southern extremity, or nearest approach to the city, is at the Fairmount Water-works, and from here it extends along both sides of the Schuylkill river for several miles, and a short distance above a cozy little village,.

ON THE WISSAHICKON DRIVE.

the Falls of the Schuylkill, where the Wissahickon Creek empties into the river. The park boundaries, leaving the Schuylkill, then betake themselves to the Wissahickon, and include that stream and both banks from its mouth nearly to its source, a distance of six miles. But the larger portion of the park is on the west side of the Schuylkill River.

The boundaries of this section of the land conform to the shape of a very irregular hump-backed triangle. the river coursing through the side which would answer for the hypothenuse, and bending, when half way through the park, well into the middle of it. The base of the triangle lies towards the city. At its three corners are the highest altitudes of the included land. The first is the old Water-works; the second, at the opposite corner of the base, is George's Hill, and the third, Chimouni, is at the apex. From each of these a view of rare beauty and wide expanse is obtained, and from the three, nearly every part of the vast territory of the park is visible, except the northern extension of the Wissahickon Park.

The boundaries of the park include about twenty-seven hundred acres of every variety of land, part of which is native forest, while the remainder has been subjected to widely different degrees of cultivation. It exhibits every phase of the picturesque, from the well-kept lawns and highly cultured garden plots, wherein have bloomed for many generations exotic plants and multitudes of rare flowers, to the roughly-tilled fields of the careless farmer. Its surface is shaped into contours more graceful than science could have conceived or art executed, while bold rugged hills toss their heads in natural pride and disdain at the idea of being restrained by plummet and line.

### DIMENSIONS OF THE PARK.

**Fairmount is** the largest park in the United States, and there is but one, of any celebrity, larger in the world. This is Windsor, one of the Royal parks in the vicinity of London, which contains three thousand acres. Central Park, New York, is less than one-third the size of Fairmount Park.

### ENTRANCE TO FAIRMOUNT.

The nearest entrance to Fairmount from the city is but a few minutes' drive from the centre of business, and is approached by several lines of street cars. To the left of the main carriage-way, on entering, are the Reservoir and the Water-works. A succession of terraces, surmounted by paths, give access to the summit of the first, whence, on account of its altitude

DRIVE ON THE WISSAHICKON, FAIRMOUNT PARK.

and peculiar position, a view of rare interest can be obtained. Close up around the base of the hill on the south, and stretching away as far as the eye can carry, is the great city. Its buildings in set ranks, its spear-like church-steeples, its waving flags, and its overhanging smoke, suggest the idea of an army entering battle—an impression that is heightened by the roar and noise that come creeping up the hill. On the near north-west, and on the east bank of the river, is the Old Park; and beyond, on the west side of the river, and also on the east, much farther than the eye can reach from this point, lie the new East and West Parks; while the Wissahickon extension is quite out of sight. The Old Park, on account of its pretty walks and cooling fountains, is still a popular resort for those who do not care to enter farther into the grounds than merely to cross their threshold. Looking back from Lemon Hill, the next point of interest, the Water-works themselves form a pleasing view, with the stretch of the river above and below the dam. Lemon Hill and Sedgeley, the neighboring estates, are points of historic interest, and the inclusion of these, and several others hereafter to be mentioned, within the park limits, by which they will for all time be preserved for the city as the absolute property of its citizens, gives an additional value to Fairmount.

### LEMON HILL.

Lemon Hill, at the close of the Revolution, was the residence of Robert Morris, the celebrated financier. It was then called "The Hills," and contained forty-five acres, which were laid out and adorned with rare taste. Here its owner hospitably entertained many of the most eminent of his compatriots; and here, in later times, it is said, when financial ruin overtook him—for while he operated for the government with signal ability, as if "sky-guarded and heaven-directed, leading to a national end by an over-ruling Providence," when acting for himself all his personal affairs went wrong and to ruin,—here he kept out of reach of sheriff's writs. At the close of the last century this fine estate passed into the hands of Henry Pratt, a merchant of liberal means and educated taste,

LEMON HILL, AND THE BOAT-HOUSES ON THE SCHUYLKILL.

under whose culture it became the pride of Philadelphia. In 1836 it was sold for a large sum to those who bought it for speculative purposes. The speculators, however, failed in their schemes, and through a commercial revulsion it came into the market at one-third its previous price, and was then purchased by the Councils for the city.

### SCHUYLKILL NAVY.

A short distance from Lemon Hill, and on the edge of the fore bay of the water-works, are the boat-houses of the "Schuylkill Navy." These buildings are erected, under licenses from the commissioners, by several clubs and by private individuals. They are models of beauty, constructed of blue and green stone, and are covered with creeping vines. Every encouragement is given to boating, and at evening in the summer the river is covered with various kinds of craft, from the capacious pleasure-boats, filled with jolly parties, to the delicate shells, in which amateur oarsmen make contests in speed up and down the stream.

The east and west banks of the Schuylkill are united just above Sedgeley by two bridges—the Girard Avenue and Connecting Railroad bridge. They cross in converging lines but at different planes, and so avoid interference.

Farther on, above "Egglesfield" is "Sweet-brier," and beyond it "Landsdowne," which perhaps, of all the historical places in the park, possesses most interest to the general public. This was the magnificent residence of John Penn, the last Colonial Governor of Pennsylvania. The mansion-like buildings, which unhappily have been destroyed by fire, were erected about 1770.

### DRIVES.

The finest drive in the West Park, is named after this old estate. It is a well-made road, which is submissively led about by the natural character and topography of the grounds. The engineers have acted wisely in seeking to find rather than make pleasing contours, and have very cleverly adapted the roads and paths to the existing surface. From a rustic bridge, picturesque itself, there is a charming view of Columbia bridge and the Schuylkill, where the lazy, graceful stream, hemmed in by grassy banks and cooled by the heavy foliage of the overhanging shade-trees, is curled up as if in an easy slumber.

MONSTER PINES.

On this drive also is a group of wonderful trees. It is a grove of five monarch pines, but these "vast pillars of glossy green," with their great heads stretching away up, and their branches spread out, and their trunks of "monumental proportions," are so big that a person at a short distance would think there were fifty instead of five. The tribes of the trees of the park are wonderful, even without these chiefs. Other cities have bought their parks and planted their trees, and then have waited for them to grow, and with their growth furnish shade. But in this instance ready-made trees were procured by incorporating forests and old estates. In Fairmount Park (and the forest borders of the Wissahickon are not included in the enumeration) the trees of large size, those between eighteen inches and twenty-seven feet in girth, number thirty-four thousand seven hundred, embracing, according to the Commissioners' report, thirty-nine genera and sixty species.

RAVINES.

In this vicinity, and just off from the Landsdowne drive, is a ravine—two or three of them, in fact—of rare beauty. Deep down below the level of the adjoining plain its recesses afford cool retreats, which are securely walled in by green terraces. These places are continually at the disposal of picnic parties, and hardly a day passes but that they are occupied. The park authorities provide a cordon of policemen who warn away intruders from the entrances and minister to the wants of the pleasure party. The efforts of the Commissioners in this respect are indicative of the light in which they regard the relation of the people to the park. They have thoughtfully sought to furnish to the masses of the people every facility of access to their property, and have only imposed such restraints to their enjoyment of it as were necessary to prevent unwarranted license. Steamboats and row-boats have been encouraged to ply on the Schuylkill, and arrangements for cheap fare and frequent trains have been made with railroads that penetrate the park. Its broad expanses of campus are the undisturbed playgrounds of the children, and no forbidding signs warn them from intruding on the grass. Croquet parties make the lawns of the old estates, where erst courtly ladies promenaded, ring again with their mirth and hilarity. The very mansions themselves, are, for an afternoon at least, the country residences of the people, and their spacious apartments and wide halls and cool verandas are thronged with private parties who find much pleasure in entertaining and being entertained. The fruits even of these places are at the disposal of

RAVINES IN WESTERN PARK.

the people, and in former times the school children of the city have been given a holiday, and afforded an opportunity to gather the nuts which by an October frost were ripened on nearly four thousand trees. On these occasions the number present was estimated to be quite sixty thousand. It being proposed to institute two park holidays, or rather holiday seasons: one in June for botanical and floral recreation, and the other in autumn for nut-gathering.

### GEORGE'S HILL.

George's Hill is perhaps, at present, the most popular of all the resorts in the park for equestrian and driving parties. It is the high point in the western base of the triangle. It was presented as a gift by Jesse George and his sister Rebecca George, subject to annuities for life, and consists of eighty-three acres. In a characteristic address accompanying the donation, Mr. George stated that the property had been the home of his ancestors for many generations, and from the first settlement of the country has retained many of its original features. With a view of preserving it to their memory very much in the same rural condition as when they occupied it, he gave it to the city, to be forever kept for park purposes. Both of the donors reserved but a small annual payment during their lifetime. A few weeks after the grand celebration which attended the opening of the drive to the newly acquired property, Rebecca George quietly passed away, and not long thereafter Jesse followed her.

### BELMONT.

An inviting drive has been run along the western summit leading from George's Hill to the grounds in front of Belmont Mansion. Belmont was the residence of Judge Peters, a magistrate who exercised his varied functions with rare wit and ability. His hospitality was proverbial, and was enjoyed by many distinguished personages, among whom was George Washington, who set out a chestnut tree on the place, which, with a line of fine hemlocks, planted one hundred and twenty years ago, and many of them covered with ivy, flourished until recently. The hemlocks, many of them are still standing. The arms of the family may yet be seen in the wainscoted principal room, and on one of the windows is a "good-bye" which some departing guest of the last century has cut with a diamond.

## TOM MOORE'S COTTAGE.

Under the bank of Belmont and nestled close to the river is the plainest kind of a plain story-and-a-half cottage, which is said to have been the residence of

HEMLOCK GLEN ON THE WISSAHICKON.

Tom Moore while in this country. It is of all places along the river the most prosaic, and we wonder that this should have attracted the attention, even for a moment, of the poet. Of it, however, he sings:—

>——"while I wing'd the hours
>Where Schuylkill winds his way through banks of flowers,
>Though few the days, the happy evenings few,
>So warm with heart, so rich with mind they flew,
>That my charmed soul forgot its wish to roam," etc.

Nearly opposite "Tom Moore's Cottage" are "Ormiston," "Belleview," and "Edgely," each invested with peculiar associations. To the grounds about these estates, also, croquet and picnic parties make frequent excursions, and relieve the hobgoblin quiet, for a wonderful ghost is said to have once been joint possessor with the old residents. In close proximity to this region, thick with places of historical interest, is a roomy house which was built by Mr. McPherson, uncle of the commander of McPherson's Blues; was afterwards the property of General Williams; but for a time had been owned by Benedict Arnold, who married Miss Shippen, the noted Philadelphia belle.

### LAUREL HILL CEMETERY.

Farther up the river is Laurel Hill Cemetery. It is like all cemeteries, with its white glistening tombs, its green turf and graveled walks and queer inscriptions. It is like all American cemeteries of to-day, with its frequent soldiers' monuments. But it differs from all others in its sleepy, dreamy appearance, and the beautiful ravines which run through it, conveying brooks with subdued murmurings to the river, and affording opportunities for nestling aeries, from which those who come to rest awhile with the dead may look out on one side over the peaceful river, and on the other toward the beautiful grounds.

### FALLS BRIDGE.

Above Laurel Hill is the Falls Bridge across the Schuylkill, and a short distance beyond, on the riverbank, is the pretty village of the Falls of the Schuylkill. It is the pleasant place of residence of many gentlemen who do business in the city, and a popular resort for driving and boating parties from Philadelphia, who come here to the "cat-fish and coffee" suppers which are delightfully served at the plain hotels of the village and in the valley of the Wissahickon. The "Falls" of the Schuylkill, however, are a myth, since the dam has covered them with water. Here and there an eddy is formed by the water hurrying around a few intruding rocks which disturb its serenity. But beyond this there is no likeness to falls, or even rapids.

The Falls of the Schuylkill, like everything else in the park, as the reader will believe by this time, are

BRIDGE OVER WISSAHICKON, NEAR MOUNT AIRY.

also celebrated in history. The annals of the ante-Revolutionary times tell us that at an early era in the eighteenth century an association called the "Society of Fort St. David," having on its list a large and respectable number of the nobility of those days, was established in this vicinity. Many of the founders of the society were Welshmen, and some were members of the Society of Friends, companions of William Penn, and co-emigrants to the New World. On an elevated and extensive rock contiguous to the eastern bank of the river, and projecting into the rapids that existed at that time, rose the primitive but convenient and strong structure of hewn timber cut from the opposite forest. It was capacious enough for the accommodation of the numerous garrison, who were then "more celebrated for their deeds of gastronomy than of arms." The building was seventy feet long and twenty feet wide, and had fourteen ascending steps in front. The sides, which consisted entirely of folding or movable doors and windows, were borne off by the Hessians for their huts in 1777-8, and the place was so changed and injured that it was never used for its former purposes, after the Revolution. In its early days it was a semi-political as well as social club, and many prominent men of the times were honored by being admitted to its membership. Its officers, who were commissioned with much form and carried high titles, ruled with supreme sway, and were, in all matters of state, implicitly obeyed. The annals of the official book give an account on the sixteenth of April, 1768, of the election to the "Colony of the Schuylkill" of a man who needed not this mark of distinction to cause him to be remembered, and yet was complimented by it. We read: "John Dickenson, Esq., the friend of Liberty, the second Pitt, and the author of the Farmers' letters, for his patriotic productions in behalf of the rights, liberties, and privileges of the present as well as the rising and future generations in America, is hereby admitted one of our members, for good services done by him to the interests of the British Plantations in America," etc.

Although the lodge at the Falls had been so much injured during the Revolution as to be untenable, the members, as many of them as could be assembled, and with accessions of loyal spirits, reorganized after the war, and for some years continued the practice of annually resorting to the neighborhood to fish and recreate.

During this time a reception was given with much

formality to General Lafayette. A grand banquet was spread and festivities of various kinds were introduced in honor of the French General and the hero of Revolutionary battles. It is related of the affair that when the mirth was at its height the distinguished guest insisted upon being provided with towels and an apron, in order that, with the celebrated men around him, he might perform his share of the domestic and culinary duties.

PRO BONO PUBLICO.

WEST LAUREL HILL CEMETERY.

Over the river, above the Falls of the Schuylkill, is West Laurel Hill Cemetery, which is, topographically speaking, on the apex of the irregular triangle which the park boundaries form. From its summit wide sweeping views of the river above and below are presented, views so attractive that they have already tempted the pencils of several artists. A glimpse is given on the opposite shore of the Wissahickon at its confluence with the Schuylkill.

Fairmount Park, in addition to the extensive lands on the east and west banks of the river, embraces, as has before been suggested, the Wissahickon Creek for six miles from its mouth, and sufficient territory on both sides to make a grand drive. A road at present runs through the valley, and has been in use for many years by residents at Chestnut Hill, a collection of handsome country places near the source of the **Wissahickon**. Although merely a country road, it is the most attractive drive out of Philadelphia, on account of the magnificent scenery which it presents.

### THE WISSAHICKON.

There are not many such streams as the Wissahickon,—none perhaps in this country, and few in the world. For several miles it picks its way daintily between two rows of high hills, down to the river, bending first one way and then another; now darting straight forward, and again lying still and quiet as if devising new mischief. Sometimes it is only a noisy brook running over pebbly bottoms, and anon a flashing cascade leaping from rock to rock with shouting noise. Then it widens out into a sober river which flows into a peaceful lake, so quiet that down in its depths the trees that meet above it are reflected with every delicate outline of foliage. After playing lake for a while, and when it can keep quiet no longer, it is off with a leap over some rustic dam, to repeat its waywardness all along its course to the Schuylkill. It is enclosed all the way by high hills whose bases creep down to the very water's edge, and whose summits are crowned with lofty peaks and craggy rocks which bristle against the sky. On their sides are—

> Majestic woods of every vigorous green
> Stage above stage, high waving o'er the hills;
> And to the far horizon wide diffused
> A boundless deep immensity of shade.

So close do the embracing hills come, as if to guard their precious charge, that it has been necessary to

cut the road into their sides, and all day long it is
shaded by their frowning heads. Here and there are

THE DEVIL'S POOL.

projecting boulders, bare and destitute of any living

thing. Near by is a quiet nook, carpeted with soft mosses and odorous with the fragrance of wild-flowers and ferns.

Romancers have woven the queer legends of the Wissahickon, which date back a couple of centuries, into interesting tales that are still read with avidity. The artists of to-day, like those of the last generation, have made its haunts their out-door studios. Many of its phases have been transferred to canvas; and others, where ruins of old mills and picturesque, odd-fashioned bridges relieve the landscape, afford studies of rare beauty.

Through the valley at frequent intervals are inns, which, until recently, were the resort of picnic parties and pleasure-seekers. The proprietors of them had procured wild animals and tamed them to exhibit to their guests. One enterprising tavern-keeper added to his collection a cage of monkeys, which entertained at all hours with their antics a group of amused spectators.

One of the most picturesque places in the valley of the Wissahickon is where Creasheim's creek runs into the larger stream. Here a pool, dark and deep, lurks under a huge overhanging rock. It is called the Devil's Pool, and the glen which surrounds it is a highly-prized resort for picnic parties, on account of its beauty and retirement.

Along the road drinking fountains have been erected, through which the pure water from the springs is conducted. They are plain but still beautiful, and are so situated as to add an additional attraction to the surrounding scenery. These bear, as do the others erected elsewhere by the city authorities, the inscription *Pro bono publico ; esto perpetua*, indicating the design and desire of their founders.

Farther on up the stream is the old bridge over the Wissahickon near Valley Green, and above it still is Indian Rock, where it is said a chieftain used to bring his people for councils of war and to give them instruction. Away on above these the stream grows smaller, and the hills, relieved of their duty of guarding it, surrender their charge to the open meadows and gentle banks, which make up a landscape of rare beauty near Chestnut Hill.

VIEW UP THE SCHUYLKILL FROM THE FALLS.

COLLEGIATE AND SCIENTIFIC DEPARTMENT
UNIVERSITY OF PENNA.
Woodland Avenue, near Chestnut Street.

# INDEPENDENCE HALL.

One of the first public buildings which will attract the attention of the stranger, and one that is most eagerly sought after, is the venerable Old State House, or Independence Hall, located on Chestnut Street, between Fifth and Sixth. It is a somewhat plain but substantial brick structure, built in 1734. It was in the east room, on the first floor of this building, that the immortal Declaration of Independence was passed by Congress, July 4th, 1776. The Hall has been dedicated to public use. A large number of portraits of Revolutionary patriots by Peale, Inman and others, have been placed upon the walls. Rush's fine statue of Washington adorns the east end of the Hall. The old chandelier used by the Continental Congress hangs in its old place. The Liberty bell, bearing the motto: "Proclaim Liberty throughout the land to all the inhabitants thereof"—and which proclaimed freedom on the first celebration of Independence, July 8th, 1776, is placed on a pedestal in the vestibule. A collection of mementoes and curiosities of the "times that tried men's souls," may be seen here. Open to all from 9 A. M. to 3 P. M.

In the upper parts of the building, the rooms once occupied by the United States Congress are now used as the Chambers of the City Councils. The other parts of the building, and the wings, are occupied as public offices and court rooms.

The present steeple, erected in 1828, is a *fac simile* of the old one, which was removed on account of its decay.

# THE UNITED STATES CUSTOM HOUSE,

Chestnut Street, between Fourth and Fifth. This building, formerly occupied by the United States bank, is a splendid marble edifice, in imitation of the Parthenon at Athens, and is one of the finest specimens of Doric architecture erected in modern times. It was com-

CUSTOM HOUSE.

menced in 1819, completed in 1824, and cost half a million dollars.

## UNITED STATES MINT,

N. W. cor. of Chestnut and Juniper, is a handsome brick building, faced with marble. Its style of architecture is an imitation of a Grecian temple of the Ionic Order. It has a front of 122 feet on Chestnut street, and extends back to Penn Square. The portico in front is 62 feet wide; and its entablature, which is of white marble, is supported by six marble columns. The main entrance is from Chestnut Street, where persons connected with the institution are in attendance to escort visitors through the establishment. Visitors are admitted every day, except Saturdays and Sundays, between 9 and 12 o'clock. All the operations, from melting the crude metal to coining. may be seen here. The operations carried on are exceedingly curious and interesting. One steam engine is said to be unsurpassed in the States for gracefulness of movement. A magnificent cabinet of coins of all ages and nations can be seen here.

## THE MERCHANTS' EXCHANGE,

Covering nearly an entire block, and fronting on three streets, Third, Walnut, and Dock. An elegant marble building, with semi-circular portico of Corinthian columns. The semi-rotunda, with a part of the main building, constitutes the great hall of the Exchange, which is now used as a reading-room

## GIRARD COLLEGE,

Situated on Ridge avenue, above Girard avenue. This magnificent building, one of the most costly in the United States, was commenced July 4, 1833, finished in 1847, and opened for educational purposes January 1, 1848. The main building is constructed of white marble, in the form of a Grecian temple of the Corinthian order, entirely surrounded by lofty columns.

The body of the building within the walls and columns is 111 feet wide, by 169 feet long, and 56 feet 8 inches high. The roof is of marble, and weighs 969½ tons. The out-buildings are

GIRARD COLLEGE.

of marble, and are very handsome. The edifice, mansion, and improvement of the grounds cost $1,933,821.78. The establishment will accommodate 500 children.— Only male orphan children are admitted.

Visitors are admitted by tickets, which may be obtained at the Mayor's office, or of any of the directors.

## UNITED STATES NAVAL ASYLUM,

Gray's Ferry road, below South street; founded 1835. The principal building is of marble, 360 feet front by 175 deep. The grounds and park contain 25 acres. There are accommodation for 400 pensioners — old seamen who have seen hard service. Visitors are admitted upon application any time during the day.

## UNITED STATES ARSENAL.

Near Frankford. A large quantity of arms, a powder magazine, trophies won in battle from the enemy, etc., may be seen here. Visitors are admitted to the buildings on application to the commanding officer.

## THE ACADEMY OF NATURAL SCIENCES,

Situated on the S. W. Cor. Nineteenth and Race. This institution was founded in January, 1812, and incorporated in 1817, for the advancement of Natural Science in all its branches. The society has a library of about 30,000 volumes, and maps, charts, periodicals, etc. The museum is the largest in the United States. It is divided into cabinets of Zoology, Botany, Geology, and Mineralogy, etc. There is a collection of crania containing several hundred specimens of human skulls. The cabinet of specimens of Ornithology is immense, numbering over 70,000 stuffed birds. The variety of humming birds is very large. In the Botanic Department are about 70,000 specimens of plants. In fact, in all branches of science this museum is complete. Visitors are admitted on Tuesday and Friday afternoons.

## THE PHILADELPHIA LIBRARY,

Corner Fifth and Library streets, is the oldest public

THE ART GALLERY or MEMORIAL HALL.

## THE PHILADELPHIA LIBRARY,

Now located in an elegant and roomy building on Locust Street, below Broad, founded by Benjamin Franklin and others, is the oldest in the city. The Loganian Free Library is connected with it. Though not a free library the directors are very liberal and permit the use of books and the reading-room to the public, any respectable person having access to them upon application. The Philadelphia Library Company is legatee and custodian of the

## RIDGEWAY LIBRARY,

Located on Broad Street. It occupies the entire block bounded by Thirteenth, Broad, Christian and Carpenter Sts. and is a magnificent building. It was founded by the late Dr. Rush, who left his entire estate of over a million dollars for its maintenance, he naming it after his wife, who was a Miss Ridgeway.

## THE MERCANTILE LIBRARY,

On Tenth, above Chestnut street. It was founded for the benefit of young men employed in the various mercantile establishments of the city, and has a large collection of well-assorted books for popular reading.

Besides the Philadelphia and Mercantile Libraries, there are several other public libraries, including—

THE GERMAN LIBRARY, Seventh, above Chestnut.

THE APPRENTICES LIBRARY, in the old Friends' meeting-house, corner Fifth and Arch.

THE FRIENDS' FREE LIBRARY, Arch, above Third.

SOUTHWARK LIBRARY, Second, below Bainbridge.

GIRARD LIBRARY, S. W. corner Sixth and Girard avenue.

JAMES PAGE FREE LIBRARY, Girard avenue, below Shackamaxon street; and

THE FRIENDS' ASSOCIATION LIBRARY.

There are also libraries connected with many of the literary, scientific, and religious associations of the city.

## PENNSYLVANIA INSTITUTION FOR THE DEAF AND DUMB,

N. W. Corner of Broad and Pine streets. This institution was founded in 1820, and the present edifice completed in 1825. The building is of granite, 96 feet front

EXCHANGE.

by 235 feet in depth. There are accommodations for about 200 pupils, who are treated with every regard for their welfare and improvement. Visitors are admitted on application to the Principal, Mr J. Foster. Public exhibitions are given in the institution on Thursday afternoons.

PENNSYLVANIA INSTITUTION FOR THE BLIND,

At the corner of Twentieth and Race. It was founded in 1833. The building is four stories high, with a front of 150 feet on Race street, with two wings of 60 feet in depth, and accommodates about 100 pupils, who are taught various avocations, and educated very thoroughly. Particular attention is paid to music; and many of the pupils become so proficient, that they are enabled to gain a livelihood by becoming organists, teachers of music, etc. Visitors are admitted on application to the Principal. Very pleasing concerts are given on Wednesday afternoons, accompanied by a full orchestra. A small admission fee (15cts.) is charged, to avoid t o great a crowd.

THE PENNSYLVANIA HOSPITAL,

On the block bounded by Eighth and Ninth, and Spruce and Pine—principal entrance on Eighth. It is surrounded by majestic trees, and exhibits considerable architectural beauty, though somewhat venerable in aspect. It was founded in 1751 by benevolent citizens of Philadelphia. Its length from east to west, is 281 feet. It consists of a centre building 64 feet front, by 61 feet deep, and two wings extending north and south at the end of long connecting wards. There are also several outbuildings. There is a fine statue of William Penn in lead on the Pine street front, which was presented to the institution by John Penn. Visitors are admitted every day between 10 A. M. and sunset, except on Saturdays and Sundays.

THE PENNSYLVANIA HOSPITAL FOR THE INSANE.

This is a branch of the Pennsylvania Hospital, and is located in West Philadelphia, between Market street and Haverford road, and Forty-second and Forty-ninth streets. The grounds, which are beautifully adorned with trees, flowers, and shrubbery, embrace 133 acres. They are divided into two parts. On each of them a hospital building has been erected, the cost of which, together with the grounds, was over $600,000. Both are built of cut stone, and have an imposing appearance. One of these buildings is devoted to the male, and the other to the female patients. They are capable of accommodating 500 insane patients. Visitors are admitted from 10 A. M. till sunset, except on Saturdays and Sundays.

## FRIENDS' ASYLUM FOR THE INSANE.

This institution is located in the northern part of the city, near Frankford. It is supported by contributions from Friends, and by pay received from patients. It is managed with eminent prudence, skill, and humanity.

## THE BLOCKLEY ALMS-HOUSE.

This is a magnificent pile of buildings situated on the west side of the Schuylkill, opposite South street. It occupies a spacious tract of land some 190 acres, belonging to the city. It has accommodations for about 2500 persons. It is built in the form of a hollow square, is three stories in height, and the buildings on each side are 500 feet in length. In the middle of the south front is an elegant portico, in the Tuscan style of architecture, with six handsome columns. There are here a very extensive hospital and insane asylum. Visitors are admitted in day time on application.

## WILLS' HOSPITAL.

This institution was founded by James Wills, who gave to the city for the purpose $108,390. Its grounds occupy the entire block bounded by Race, Cherry, Eighteenth and Nineteenth streets. It is devoted to the treatment of diseases of the eye and limbs. Besides the inmates, many of whom are charity patients, there are numerous "out patients" who attend for advice and relief. Logan Square is directly opposite on the other side of Race street, and adds

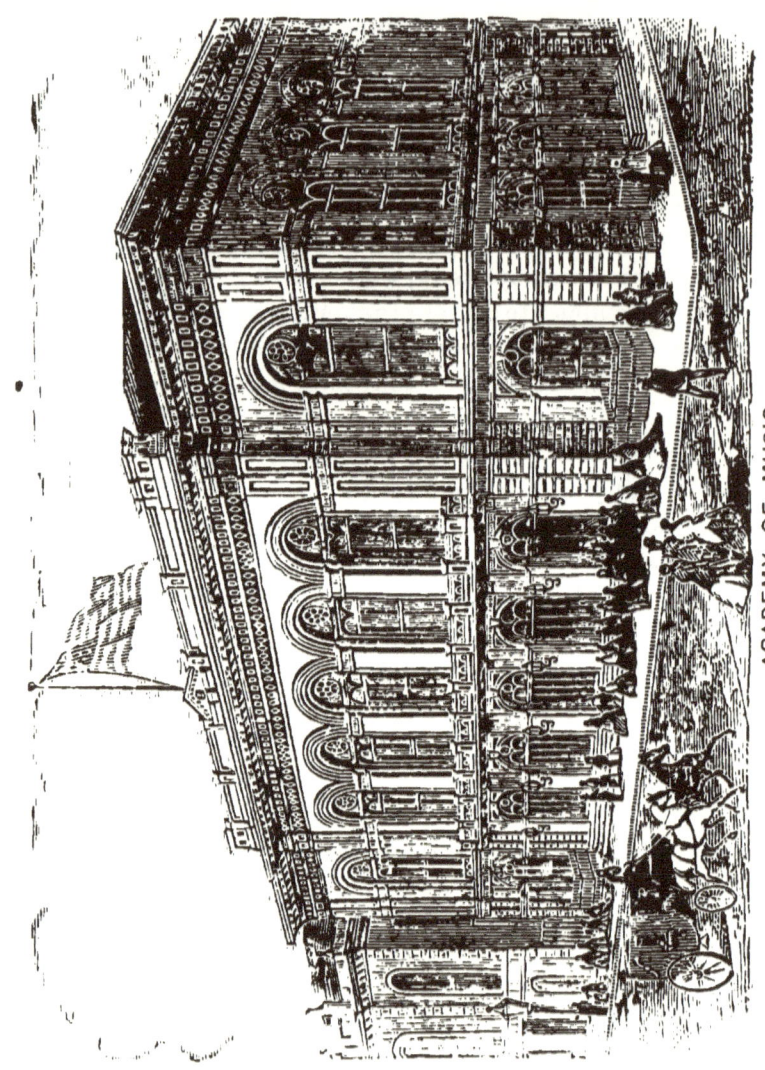
ACADEMY OF MUSIC,
Broad and Locust.

much to the desirability of its location. Visitors are admitted on application to the Steward.

## HOUSE OF INDUSTRY,

On Catharine above Seventh. This location is in the midst of the lowest and most destitute portion of the population. The object of the institution is to afford employment, with occasional shelter and relief, to the needy.

## THE EASTERN PENITENTIARY,

Of the State of Pennsylvania, is located on Coates street, near Fairmount Park. The front is of granite, and resembles in appearance a baronial castle of the Feudal times. It was finished in 1829. The number of prisoners is about 500. The system of confinement is separate, but not solitary. The cells radiate from a common centre—each prisoner having his apartment, and a small yard or enclosure. Visitors can obtain tickets of admission from the Mayor of the city, or from any of the inspectors.

## MOYAMENSING PRISON,

Is on Passyunk avenue, near Tenth. It is constructed of Quincey granite, in the Tudor-Gothic style of architecture. The front of the prison consists of a square building, in the centre, three stories in height, with a wing on each side, flanked by octagonal towers. The wings are two stories in height, and contain the gates of the prison yard.

There is a separate prison for females, to which the entrance is on Eleventh street. There are 400 cells for males, and 100 for female prisoners. Permits can be obtained at the Mayor's office, corner Fifth and Chestnut streets.

## THE HOUSE OF REFUGE,

Is at the corner of Twenty-second and Poplar streets, near the western end of Girard College grounds, and a little north of the State Penitentiary. It is intended for the restraint and reclamation of youthful offenders against the laws, and a home for those whose neglected and vagrant condition renders them liable to be led into crime. It is built

ACADEMY OF FINE ARTS,
On Broad St., cor. Cherry.

of brick, and embraces numerous improvements in its various arrangements. It is spacious, well ventilated, and warmed, being heated by steam, and presents throughout an aspect of order, neatness and comfort. Originally built by private liberality, it has been recognized by an Act of the State Legislature, and authorized to receive and detain juveniles committed to their custody by the magistrates and courts. The inmates are educated both physically and mentally, and many of them are placed in good situations, or are bound out as apprentices to suitable masters. The sexes and colors are separated, and a classification is made of the good and the bad. Visitors are admitted with tickets, which may be had of any of the Board of Managers.

## THE SCHOOL OF DESIGN FOR WOMEN

Was established in 1850, under the patronage of the Franklin Institute. Here females are instructed in drawing and other arts, at a moderate charge, with a view of benefiting the condition of the sex, by affording suitable and pleasant employment, and at the same time of improving the products of American manufactures, in those branches where artistic taste and skill are required. It is located on North Broad Cor. Master Sts. Visitors admitted on Monday from 10 A. M. to 12 M.

## THE NEW POST-OFFICE,

A magnificent and commodious building, erected for the accommodation of the U. S. Courts and the Main Post-Office of the City, centrally located on Ninth St. it occupies the entire square between Chestnut and Market. It is five stories high and has three fronts, those on Chestnut and Market being of similar design. Whilst there are entrances on each street, that on Ninth is the principal one. A fine dome surmounts the Ninth St. front, midway between Chestnut and Market, which gives the building an elegant architectural finish.

## THE UNIVERSITY OF PENNSYLVANIA,

Including the Medical College and Law School and Towne Scientific School, is located on Woodland Avenue below Walnut. The buildings are built of green stone.

## THE CENTRAL HIGH SCHOOL,

At the corner of Broad and Green streets, is a large and handsome building, with an extensive chemical laboratory, astronomical observatory, etc.

## ATHENÆUM BUILDING,

Corner of Sixth and Adelphi streets. The Historical Society of Pennsylvania occupy rooms in this building, and have an interesting museum and library. Open every Monday from 8 A. M. to 10 P. M., except during July and August.

## FAIRMOUNT WATERWORKS,

On the Schuylkill River, north of Morris street. The Fairmount Works were commenced in 1819, in consequence of the inability of the city works, built in the year 1799, to supply the wants of a growing population. This beautiful place has always been an unfading object of attraction and interest to all visitors to the city. The natural beauties of the place have been skilfully improved by art. The works situated here were for many years the only means of artificial supply of water to the city, and are still the principal means, although there are four other waterworks for different parts of the city. At Fairmount the only power used for forcing the water up to reservoirs on the hill, and at Corinthian avenue, is the water-power formed by the dam and waterfall constructed across the Schuylkill at this place.

## THE SCHUYLKILL WATER WORKS

Are situated near the Girard avenue entrance to the Park, on the east side of the Schuylkill. These works are driven by steam-power, and were originally designed to supply the old districts of Spring Garden and Penn with water. They are now connected with the general system for the whole city. These with four other works, located in different parts of the city, furnish the water for the entire municipality.

## THE GAS WORKS

Are very complete and extensive, the two principal ones are situated on the Schuylkill River, one at Point Breeze and the other at Market St.

COLUMBIA BRIDGE OVER THE SCHUYLKILL.

UNION LEAGUE CLUB HOUSE,
Cor. Broad and Sansom.

## BENEVOLENT INSTITUTIONS.

In nearly all the following places of interest visitors are admitted at all times upon application to the officers.

HOSPITALS, DISPENSARIES, AND INFIRMARIES.

Charity Hospital, 1326 Butonwood.

City (Small Pox) Hospital, Hart Lane and Lamb Tavern road.

Christ Church Hospital, Belmont avenue; office, 517 Locust.

Episcopal Hospital, Front street, Huntingdon and Lehigh avenue.

Friends' Asylum for the Insane, Frankford.

German Hospital, Twentieth and Norris.

Germantown Dispensary, Germantown av., opposite Haines.

Hahnemann Medical Dis-

HORTICULTURAL HALL.
(Centennial Building.)

pensary, Tenth above Market.

Howard Hospital and Infirmary for Incurables, 1518 Lombard.

Hospital for Inebriates, (Citizens' Association,) office, 800 Arch.

Jewish Hospital, Haverford road, near Fifty-sixth.

Lying-in Charity (Philadelphia), 126 N. Eleventh.

Lying-in Department (Northern Dispensary), 603 Spring Garden.

Northern Dispensary for Medical Relief of Poor, 603 Spring Garden.

Philadelphia Dispensary, 127 S. Fifth.

Preston Retreat, (Lying-in Charity Hospital,) Hamilton and Twentieth.

St. Joseph's Hospital, Girard avenue and Seventeenth.

St. Mary's Hospital, 1567 Palmer.

Southern Dispensary, 318 Bainbridge.

Catholic Home for Destitute Orphan Girls, Race, ab. Seventeenth.

Children's Day Nursery, (for the care of infant children of working women while the mothers are out at work,) Blight street, bel. Pine.

Church Home for Children, Twenty-second and Pine.

Colored Orphans' Shelter, Forty-fourth and Haverford road.

Foster Home, College av. and Twenty-fourth.

Home for Aged and Infirm Colored Persons, Lombard, ab. Seventh.

Home for Destitute Colored Children, Darby road and Forty-sixth.

Home for Little Wanderers, Bainbridge, bet. Eighth and Ninth.

Home for Aged and Infirm Israelites, Haverford road and Westminster avenue.

House of the Good Shepherd, (for the reformation of unfortunate females,) Twenty-second, near Walnut.

House of Industry, Catharine, between Seventh and Eighth.

Howard Institution, (for reformation of female prisoners,) Poplar, ab. Sixteenth.

Industrial Home, Tenth, bel. Fitzwater.

Jewish Foster Home, Fifteenth, ab. Master.

Lincoln Institution, (home for boys and soldiers' orphans,) Eleventh, bel. Spruce.

Little Sisters of the Poor,

Fifteenth, near Columbia avenue.

Lutheran Orphan Home, 5582 Germantown av.

Midnight Mission, (for reformation of abandoned women,) Locust, ab. Ninth.

Newsboys' Home, on Sixth above Spruce.

Northern Home for Friendless Children, Brown and Twenty-third.

Old Man's Home, Thirty-ninth and Powelton av.

Orphans' Home of the Shepherds of the Lambs, Bridesburg.

Pennsylvania Industrial Home for Blind Women, Locust, ab. 39th, (W. P.)

Philadelphia Orphan Society's Asylum, Eighteenth and Cherry.

Sailors' Home, Front, bel. Pine.

St. John's Orphan Asylum, Westminster av. and Forty-ninth.

St. Joseph's Orphan Asylum for Girls, S. W. cor. Seventh and Spruce.

St. Vincent's Home, (destitute infants,) Eighteenth and Wood.

St. Vincent's Orphan Asylum, near Tacony.

Soldiers' Home, Sixteenth and Filbert.

Temporary Home Association for Girls, Filbert, ab. 7th.

Union Temporary Home for Friendless Children, Poplar, ab. Fifteenth.

West Philadelphia Children's Home, 199 N. Forty-first.

## PUBLIC SQUARES.

The Public Squares are numerous, and very ornamental to the city. They are laid out with well-kept walks, majestic trees, green and luxuriant grass plots, and some having beautiful fountains. On pleasant days in the spring and summer, they are filled with happy people, principally women and children, seated on the pleasant shady seats, or promenading under the trees, enjoying the pure and refreshing air. As they resemble each other in their general features, it is only necessary to give the names and locations of the more important ones.

INDEPENDENCE SQUARE, Between Fifth, Sixth, Chestnut and Walnut streets, was formerly the property of the

SCENE IN WEST LAUREL HILL CEMETERY.

State, and was conveyed to the city with the proviso, that it should be kept open as a public square.

## WASHINGTON SQUARE

Is west of Sixth, and south of Walnut. It was formerly a "Potter's" field, or graveyard for paupers, but is now one of the finest of the public squares.

## FRANKLIN SQUARE

Is between Sixth, Vine, Race, and Franklin streets. A handsome square, with a beautiful fountain in the centre.

## LOGAN SQUARE,

Bounded by Race, Vine, Eighteenth and Nineteenth streets.

## RITTENHOUSE SQUARE,

Between Walnut, Locust, Eighteenth and Nineteenth streets. In the neighborhood of these last two squares are many elegant private residences.

## PENN SQUARE

Is situated at Broad and Market streets. The court house and offices of the officers of the city and county are being erected here. It was so intended by William Penn, and in accordance with the wishes of the majority of the citizens, who wisely voted in favor of it.

## NORRIS SQUARE,

Given to the city by Isaac Parker Norris, is bounded by Susquehanna avenue and Hancock, Diamond and Howard streets.

## JEFFERSON SQUARE,

West from Third, and south from Washington avenue.

## CEMETERIES.

The Cemeteries of Philadelphia are noted for their rural and picturesque beauty, the good taste of the monuments, and the pains taken to render them beautiful and attractive.

## LAUREL HILL

Is one of the most beautiful in this country. It is situated west of Ridge avenue, and on the east side of the Schuylkill River, just below the Falls. The entrance is built of brown stone, of Doric style, the entablature being supported by eight fluted columns. Within the grounds are a Gothic chapel, the superintendent's residence, an observatory, commanding a fine view of the river and opposite shore; a hot house, for flowers and shrubbery, etc. Many distinguished people are buried here, and elegant and costly monuments abound.

## WEST LAUREL HILL CEMETERY,

Situated on the west bank of the Schuylkill River, beyond the Falls. This is a new cemetery, and presents many advantages. It is accessible by Reading Railroad, Ridge avenue horse cars, and the Germantown and Norristown Railroad.

## WOODLAND CEMETERY

Is situated on the west bank of the Schuylkill, below the Chestnut street bridge. Entrance on Woodland avenue, or Darby road.

## MOUNT VERNON CEMETERY

Is adjacent to Laurel Hill Cemetery, on the opposite side of Ridge road.

## MOUNT PEACE CEMETERY

Adjoins Mount Vernon Cemetery on the north.

## GLENWOOD CEMETERY

Is at the corner of Ridge avenue and Islington lane, about a mile north-west of Girard College.

## THE ODD FELLOWS' CEMETERY

Is a little north of Glenwood, on Islington lane.

## MONUMENT CEMETERY

Is on Broad street, above Montgomery.

## OLD OAK CEMETERY,

On Nicetown lane, between Twenty-third and Twenty-seventh streets.

## NEW CATHEDRAL CEMETERY,

Third street, between Nicetown lane and Luzerne street.

## CATHEDRAL CEMETERY,

Forty-eighth street, between Wyalusing street and Girard avenue.

# CHURCH DIRECTORY.

The usual Sabbath Services are held at 10½ A. M., 3½ and 7½ P. M. from May to October, the rest of the year 8 P. M. All have morning, some afternoon and others evening, whilst a few have all three services where other hours are used they are designated by figures.

**ADVENT CHRISTIAN.**
Twenty-fifth & Huntingdon
2d Advent, 7th, bel. Poplar
**BAPTIST.**
Angora, 58th & Baltimore av.
Berean, Chestnut, ab. 40th
Beth Eden, Broad & Spruce
Bethany, Fox Chase
Bethesda, 5th & Venango
Blockley, 53d, ab. Haverford av.
Broad St., Broad & Brown
Bustleton Chapel, Bustleton
Byberry Chapel, Byberry
Calvary, 5th & Carpenter
Centennial, 23d & Oxford
Chestnut Hill, Main & Summit
East, Hanover ab. Girard av.
Eleventh, 12th ab. Race
Falls of Schuylkill, Green
Fifth, 18th & Spring Garden
Fiftieth, 7th & Susquehanna av
First, Broad & Arch
First German, 6th, ab. Poplar
First, Price, nr. Main (Gtn.)
First, Green la. (Myk.)
First, 36th & Chestnut (W. P.)
Fourth, 5th & Buttonwood
Frankford, Paul & Unity
Frankford & Aramingo
Gethsame, 18th & Columbia av
Grace, Berk & Mervine
Haverford av. & Westminster
Holmesburg, Main st.
Immanuel, 23d & Summer
Lower Dublin, nr. Bustleton
Manataura, Roxborough
Mantua, 40th & Silverton av.
Mariners, Front, bel. Christian
Memorial, Broad & Master
Messiah, Dauphin, N. Amber
Milestown, Oak la.
Mt. Olive, 17th & Poplar
Nicetown, Gtn. av.
North, 8th, ab. Master
Olivet, 6th & Federal
Passyunk av., ab. Broad
Pilgrim, 23d & Christian
Roxborough, Ridge av.
Second, 7th, ab. Poplar
Second, Main & Upsal (Gtn.)
Second German, 2d, ab. Norris
South, Broad & Reed
Spring Garden, 13th, ab.Wallace
Spruce St., ab. 4th
Tabernacle, Chestnut, ab. 18th
Truth, 8th, ab. Green
Third, 2d, ab. Catherine
Third, Wister St (Gtn.)
**BAPTIST, (Colored.)**
First African, Cherry, ab. 10th
Enon, Coulter St (Gtn.)
Oak St., 41st & Ludlow
Shiloh, Clifton & South
**BIBLE CHRISTIAN.**
Christ, 3d, ab. Girard av
**CHILDREN OF ZION.**
Congregation, Pine, ab. 2d
**CHRISTADELPHIANS.**
Fortieth bel. Market
**CHRISTIAN, (Independent.)**
First,Marlborough,ab.Belgrade
Mt. Zion, Christian, ab. 5th
**CHURCH OF THE BRETHREN.**
Marshall, ab. 12th
Main. ab. Shapneck (Gtn.)
**CHURCH OF GOD.**
Arch & 13th
Union Bethel, Gtn. av. & Berks
**CONGEGATIONAL.**
Central, 18th & Green
**CONGREGATIONAL, (Independent.)**
Trinity, Frankford
**DISCIPLES OF CHRIST.**
First, 12th ab. Wallace
Second, Frankford av.& Adams
Third, Holly, ab. Aspen
**EVANGELICAL.**
Christ, 8th ab. Poplar
Emanuel, 4th, bel. Poplar

Southwark, 5th ab. Carpenter
John, 6th & Dauphin
Zion, Thompson, (Bdg.)
Zion, Rittenhouse, (Gtn.)
FRIENDS, (Orthodox.)
Beach St. & Fairmount av
Fourth & Arch,5th day,10 a.m.
Orange, ab.7th,10 a.m.&3 p.m.
Forty-Second & Powelton av.,
Main & Coulter, (Gtn.)10 a. m.
Twelth,bel.Eleventh,10½ a.m.
Orthodox St. & Penn, (Fkd.)
FRIENDS.
Byberry, 23d Ward. 10 a. m.
Girard av.&17th,3d days,10 a.m.
Green & 4th, 5th day, 10 a. m.
Race ab. 15th, 4th day, 10½ a. m.
SchoolSt.(Gtn.),4th day,10½a.m.
Spruce & 9th, 5th day, 10½ a. m.
Thirty-Fifth & Lancaster av
FRIENDS, (Primitive.)
Olive, ab. 11th, 4th day, 10 a. m.
HEBREWS.
Adath Jeshwim Juliana 9½ & 5
Anshe Emeth, New Market, ab.
Poplar, 9 a. m. & sunset
Beth-El-Emeth, Franklin, ab.
Green, summer, 9½ a. m., 8
p. m., winter, 10 a.m.,& 5 p.m.
House of Israel, Crown ab. Race
Friday,6 p.m.Saturday,9 a.m.
Hospital, Olney road, 9 a. m. &
sunset
Keneseth Isreal, 6th ab. Brown
10 a. m. & sunset
Kra-Kaner-Beth-Elohim,Pine,ab.
4th, 8½ a. m.
Mikhoe Israel, 7th, ab. Arch, 9
a. m. & sunset
Rodef Shalom, Broad & Mt. Vernon, Friday. sunset, Saturday
9½ a. m.
LATTER DAY SAINTS.
Anti-Polygamous, 9th & Callowhill
Polygamous, Pine. ab. 3d
LUTHERAN.
English, (General Council.)
Advent, 5th bel. Norris
Christ, Main st. (C. H.)
Holy Communion, Broad & Arch
St. John, Race, ab. 5th
St. Luke, 4th, bel. Thompson
St. Mary, Spring Garden,ab.13th
St. Michael, Main St. (Gtn.)
St. Paul, 22d, ab, Columbia av
St. Peters, 8th & Reed
St.Stephen,Powelton av.ab,39th
Trinity, Passyunk av. nr. 18th
German, (General Council.)
Emanuel, 4th & Capenter
Evangelical, Martin, (Rxb.)
Holy Trinity, 16th, nr. Venango

Immanuel, Plum, (Fkd.)
St. Jacobus, 3d & Columbi av
St. Johannes, 15th, Poplar
St. Michael, Trenton av
St. Paul, St. John & Brown
St. Peter, 42d & Myrtle
St. Thomas, Herman, (Gtn.)
Zion, Franklin, ab. Race
Engiisn (General Synod.)
Calvary, 4 d & Aspen
Grace, 35th & Spring Garden
Messiah, 16th & Jefferson
St. Matthew,Broad & Mt.Vernon
Trinity, Main & Queen, (Gtn.)
INDEPENDENT.
Emanuel, 4th, ab, Brown
St. Paul, 4th, bel. Canal
MENNONITE.
First, Diamond, ab. 5th
Germantown, Main, (Gtn.)
METHODIST EPISCOPAL.
Alleghany av. & Broad
Aramingo, Frankford av. & Ontario
Arch St. & Broad
Asbury, Chestnut, ab. 32d
Belmont, 43d & Aspen
Bethany, 11th & Mifflin
Bridesburg, Kirkbride (Bdg.)
Broad & Christian
Bustleton on the Pike
Cambria. bel. Kensington av
Centenary,41st & Spring Gard'n
Central, Vine ab. 12th
Central, Frankford
Central, Roxborough
Christ, 38th & Hamilton
Christian St. ab. 24th
Cohocksink, Gtn. av. ab 4th
Cookman, 12th, & Lehigh av.
Cumberland St. & Coral
East Montgomery av & Fkd. av
Ebenezer, Manyunk
Eden, Lehigh av. ab. 4th
Eighteenth St. & Wharton
Eleventh St. bel. Carpenter
Emanuel, 25th & Brown
Emory, Callowhill ab. 18th
Epworth, 56th & Race
Falls of Schuylkill
Fifth St. bel. Green
First German, Girard av.ab,12th
Fitzwater, ab. 19th
Fletcher, 54th & Paschal
Fortieth St. & Sansom
Frankford av & Folkrod
Franklinvilie, 5th & Erie av.
Front St. & Laurel
Grace, Broad & Master.
Green St. ab. 10th
Haddington, 63d & Hamtlton
Haines St., (Gtn.)
Hancock St., ab. Girard av

OLD SWEDISH CHURCH,
Swanson Street.

Kensington, Marlborough
Main St., Richmond
Marriners, Washington av. ab. 2d
Memorial, 8th & Cumberland
Messiah, Moyamensing av. & Morris
Milestown, York av. & 71st
Mt. Carmel, Gtn. av. ab. Broad
Mt. Olivet, Venango, bel. Richmond
Mt. Pleasat av. Germantown
Mt. Zion, Green la. (Myk.)
Nazareth, 13th, ab. Race
Nineteenth & Poplar
Norris sq., Mascher & Davis
Orthodox St. & Tacony av (Fkd.)
Park av. & Norris
Pitman, 23d & Lombard
Port Richmond, Richmond, ab. Ann
Ridge av. Roxborough
Salem, Lombard & Juniper
Sanctuary, 5th, bel. Girard av.
Scott, 8th, ab. Tasker
Sepviva St., ab. Huntingdon
Siloam, Otis, ab. Thompson
Spring Garden St., & 20th
St. George, 4th & New
St. John, 3d, ab. Beaver
St. Paul, Catherine, ab. 6th
St. Stephen, Germantown
Summerfield, Dauphin & Tulip
Tabernacle, 11th ab. Jefferson
Tacony, Tulip ab. Tyson
Tasker, 5th & Snyder av
Tioga St. & 19th
Trinity, 16th ab. Wallace
Twelfth, St. & Ogden
Twentieth St. & Jefferson
Twenty-ninth & York
Union, 4th bel. Arch
Westley Chapel, Chestnut Hill
Western, 20th, bel. Walnut
Wharton St. ab. 3d
York St. & Holman

**METHODIST EPISCOPAL**
(Colored.)
Berean, 20th & Heman
John Wesley, 8th & Bainbridge
Oxford St., bel. Paul, (Fkd.)
Zoar, Brown ab. 4th

**METHODIST (Independent.)**
Brandywine ab 15th
Ridge av. ab. Columbia av.
Wesley, Clearfield & Frankford

**METHODIST EPISCOPAL.**
(African.)
Allen Chapel, 19th & Lombard
Bethel, Centre, (Gtn.)
Bethel, 6th & Lombard
Campbell Chapel, Frankford
Little Wesley, Hurst
Mt. Pisgah, Locust, ab. 40th

Union, Fairmount av. ab. 4th
Zion, 7th ab. Tasker

**MORAVIANS.**
First, Franklin & Wood
Fifth, Gtn. av. ab. Dauphin
Fourth, Hancock, ab. Dauphin
Second, Franklin & Thompson
Third, Harrowgate

**NEW JERUSALEM.**
(Swedenborgian.)
Cherry an. 20th
First, 22d & Chestnut
Frankford, Paul & Unity

**PRESBYTERIAN.**
Alexander, 19th & Green
Am. Carmichael, 5th & Erie
Arch St. ab 10th
Bethany, 22d & Bainbridge
Bethesda, Frankford av. & Vienna
Bethlehem, Broad & Diamond
Calvary, Locust ab. 15th
Central, Broad, bel. Brown
Chambers, Broad Sansom
Chapel, 27th & Hagert
Chapel, 20th & Norris
Clinton St. & 10th
Cohocksink, Franklin & Columbia av.
Eastburn Mariners, Front, & Pine
Falls of Schuylkill, Ridge av
Fifteenth St., & Lombard
First, 7th & Locust
First, Bridesburg
First, Perkiomen, (C. H.)
First, Chelton av. (Gtn.)
First Kensington, Girard Av., ab Hanover
First Manayunk, Centre St.
First Northern Liberties, Buttonwood ab 5th
First Southwark, German ab. 2d
Fourth, 2d & Lombard
Frankford Ave, Frankford
Gaston Street, nr. Huntingdon
Gethsemane, 29th & Passyunk
Grace, 22d & Federal
Green Hill, Girard Ave. ab. 16th
Greenwich St. bel. Moya av.
Hermon, Frankford av & Harrison
Holland, Federal ab 13th
Hope Chapel, 33d & Wharton
Howard, Bainbridge ab 3d
Kenderton, 16th & Tioga
Kensington, Frankford av. ab Girard Ave
Lehigh av. ab. 5th
Mantua, Preston & Aspen
Market Square, (Gtn.)
Memorial, 18 & Montgomery av
Mount Airy.

Ninth, 16th & Sansom.
Horth 6th ab Green
North Broad St & Green
Northminster, 36th & Baring
Tenth St. bel Girard av
Northwestern, 19th & Master
Olivet, 22d & Mt. Vernon
Oxford, Broad & Oxford
Princeton, powelton av & 39th
Richmond st. ab. William
Roxborough, Ridge av
Scotts, Spruce ab. 3d
Second, 21st & Walnut
Second, Tulpehoucken (Gtn.)
Vine st. & 63d
South st. ab 11th
South Third bel. Federal
Southwestern, 20th & Fitzwater
Spring Garden, 11th bel. Green
Tabernacle, Broad ab. Chestnut
Taber, 18th & Christian
Temple, Franklin & Tennyson
Tenth, 12th & Walnut
Third, 4th & Pine
Trinity, Franklin & Cambria
Union, 13th & Spruce
Wakefield, Gtn ave, Gtn
Walnut St, ab, 39th
West Arch St & 18th
Westminster, Broad & Fitswater
West Park, Lancaster Av ab 51st
West Spruce St, & 17th
Wharton St. & 9th
Woodland, 42d & Pine
York St. ab. Coral

**PRESBYTERIAN—Colored.**
Berean, 17th & Fairmount av
Central, Lombard ab. 8th

**PROTESTANT EPISCOPAL.**
All Saints, 12th & Fitzwater
Burd's Asylum Chapel, 63d & Market 10½ A. M. and 5 P. M.
Calvary, Manheim & Paluski (Gtn) 10 A. M.; 4 P. M.
Calvery Monumental, 41st ab. Aspen, 10½ A. M. and 3 P. M.
Christ, 2d ab. Market
Christ Ch. Chapel, 20th bel Pine, 11 A. M., 4 P. M.
Christ, Tulpehocken (Gtn)
Christ, 6th & Venango
Church of the Advent, York av. & Buttonwood
Church of the Ascension, Lombard ab. 11th
Church of the Atonement, 17th & Summer. 10½ A. M., 4 P. M
Church of the Beloved Disciples, Columbia av. ab. 20th
Church of the Covenant, Filbert ab. 17th, 10½ 4
Church of the Crucifiction, 8th ab Bainbridge. 10½ A.M, 4 P.M
Church of the Epiphany, 15th & Chestnut
Church of the Evangelist, Catherine, ab 7th
Church of the Good Shepherd, Cumberland bel. Frankford
Church of the Holy Apostles, 21st & Christian
Church of the Holy Comforter, 48th & Haverford av
Church of the Holy Innocents, Tacony
Church of the Holy Trinity, 19th & Walnut
Church of the Incarnation, Broad & Jefferson
Church of the Mediator, 19th & Lombard
Church of the Messiah, Broad & Federal
Church of the Messiah, Huntingdon & Edgemont
Church of the Nativity, 11th & Mt. Vernon
Church of the Merciful Saviour, Norris & Camac
Church of the Redeemer, Front & Queen
Church of the Redemption, 22d & Callowhill
Church of the Resurrection. Broad & Tioga
Church of San Sauveur, (French) 21st ab Chestnut, 9½ A. M., 4. P. M.
Church of the Saviour, 38th bel. Market
Church of the Transfiguration, 34th & Walnut
Emanual, Marlborough
Emanual, Holmesburg
Gloria Dei, (Old Swedes) Swanson bel Christian
Grace. 12th & Cherry,
Grace, Mt. Airy, (G.n)
Holy Trinity, 22d & Spruce
St. Albans, Roxborough
St. Ambrose, 26th & Poplar
St. Andrews' 8th ab Spruce
St. Andrews' 36th bel Baring
St. Barnabas, 65th & Hamilton
St. Bartholamew, 19th Ward
St. Chrysostom, Ridge & Susquehanna ave. 10½ A. M., 4 P. M.
St. Clements, 20th & Cherry. 7, 8, 9½, 10¾ A. M., 4. 7½ P. M.
St. Davids, Centre (Myk)
St. Georges, Hazel Av & 61st 9. 10¾ A. M., and 7½ P. M.
St. James, 22d & Walnut. 10½ A. M., and 4 P. M.
St. James the Less, Nicetown av

St. James, 52d & Kershaw av
St. James, woodland av., ab. 68th
St. Johns, Brown ab 2d.
St. Johns Free Church, (Fkd)
St. John the Baptist, Mehle (Gtn), 7, 10½ A. M., 4. 7½ P. M.
St. John the Evangelist, 3d & Reed
St. Jude, Franklin ab. Brown
St. Lukes, 13th bel. Spruce.
St. Lukes, Bustleton.
St. Lukes, Main (Gtn) 10½ A M. and 4 P. M.
St. Marks, Locust, ab. 16th, 9, 10½ A. M., 7½ P. M.
St. Mary, Locust, ab. 39th
St. Matthias, 19th & Wallace
St. Matthew, Girard av. & 18th
St. Michael, High, (Gtn.)
St. Paul, 3d, ab. Spruce
St. Paul, Chestnut av. (C. H.)
St. Paul, Kensington av., nr. Buckius
St. Peters, 3d & Pine, 7¼, 10½ a. m., 4 p. m.
St. Peter, Wayne, (Gtn.)
St. Philip, Spring Garden, ab. 13th
St. Thomas, (African), 5th, ab. Locust
St. Timothy, Reed, ab. 7th
St. Timothy, Ridge av. (Myk.) 7, 9, 10½ a. m., 4, and 6 p.m.
St. Stephen, 10th, ab. Chestnut, 10½ a. m., 4, and 6 p. m.
St Stephen, Bridge, Bdg.)
Trinity, Catherine, ab. 2d
Trinity, Oxford rd., nr. 2d
Trinity, 42d bel. Kingsessing av.
Zion, 8th & Columbia av.

### REFORMED CHURCH IM AMERICA.
(Dutch Reformed.)
First, 7th & Spring Garden
Fifth, Otis, ab. Memphis
Fourth. Cotton, (Myk.)
Second, 7th ab. Brown

### REFORMED CHURCH IN THE UNITED STATES.
Bethlehem, Norris & Blair
Christ, Green, nr. 16th
Emanuel, 38th & Baring
Emanuel, Weisert, (Bdg.)
First, Race, ab. 3d
Heidleberg, 18th & Oxford
Salem, Fairmount av. ab. 3d
St. Johns, Haverford ab. 40th
St. Marks, 5th, ab. Huntingdon
St. Paul, 17th & Fitzwater
Trinity, 7th, ab. Oxford
Zion, 6th, bel. Thompson

### REFORMED EPISCOPAL.
Holy Trinity, 12th & Oxford
Our Redeemer, 16th & Oxford
Covenant, Melon, ab. 12th
Emanuel, York and Sepviva
Frankford av.,Co-operative Hall
Grace, Falls of Schuylkill
Reconciliation, 13th and Tasker
Second, Chestnut, ab. 21st
St. Paul, Orthodox, (Fkd.)
Third. Wayne, (Gtn).

### REFORMED PRESBYTERIAN.
(General Synod.)
First. Chestnut and 18th
First, Broad ab. Pine, 10½, & 4.
Fifth, Front, ab. York, 10½ & 3½
Fourth, 18th and Filbert, 10½ & 3
Second, 22d, ab. Vine, 10½ & 3
Second,20th and Vine,10½ & 3½
(Synod.)
First, 17th and Bainbridge, 10½ a. m., 4 p. m.
Second, 17th, ab. Arch, 10½ a. m., 3½ p. m.
Third, Deaf bel. Frankford av. 10½ a. m., 3 p. m.

### ROMAN CATHOLIC.
Cathedral of St. Peter & St. Paul. 18th and Race, 6, 7½, 8½, 9, 10½, a. m.
All Saints, Bockius, (Bdg.), 8, 10 a. m., 2 and 3 p. m.
Annunciation, 10th and Dickerson, 6½, 8, 10½, a. m., 3 p. m.
Assumption, Spring Garden, ab. 11th,6,7½,9, 0½ a.m., 3½ p.m.
Assumption of the Blessed Virgin. Oak, (Myk), 7, 8½, 10½, 3½
Church of the Gesu, 18th and Stiles. 6,7, 7½, 7¾, 8, 9, 10, 3½
Holy Trinity, (German), 6th and Spruce, 7, 8, 9, 0½, 2½
Immaculate Conception, Front and Canal, 6, 8½, 10½, 3½
Our Lady of Consolation, Chestnut av., (C. H.). 8, 10½, 4
Our Lady of the Visitation, Front and Lehigh av., 6½, 8½, 10½ a. m., 3½ p. m.
Our Mother of Sorrows, 48th and Decatur av., 7½, 10½, 3½
Sacred Heart of Jesus, 3d bel. Reed, 6½,8½,10½ a.m.7½p.m.
St. Agatha, 38th and Spring Garden, 6½, 8, 10½ a m., 3½ p.m.
St. Alphonsus, 4th and Reed,7½, 10 a. m.; 2½ p. m.
St. Ann, Lehigh av. and Cedar, 3½, 6½, 8, 8½, 9, 10½ 3½
St. Augustine, 4th, ab. Race, 6, 8, 9, 10½ a. m., 3½ p. m.
St. Boniface, Diamond and Norris sqr., 5½, 7¼, 9, 10 3, 7½

St. Bridget, Falls of Schuylkill, 8, 10½ a. m., 3½ p. m.
St. Charles Borromeo, 20th and Christian, 6, 7½, 8½, 9, 10½ a. m., 3¼ p. m.
St. Clement, 71st and Woodland av., 7½, 10½ a. m., 3½ p. m.
St. Dominic, Holmesburg, 7½, 10½ a. m., 3½ p. m.
St. Edward the Confessor, 8th & York, 7, 8, 9, 10½ a. m., 3½ p.m.
St. Elizabeth, 23d and Berks, 6½, 8½, 10½ a. m., 3½ p. m.
St. Francis Xavier, 25th and Biddle, 6½, 8, 8½, 10½ 3½
St. James, 3 th Chestnut, 6½, 7½, 8½, 9½, 10½ a. m., 4 p.m.
St. Joacbism, Penn and Pine, (Fkd.), 7, 9, 10½ a. m., 3½ p.m.
St. John the Baptist, Robinson, (Myk.) 6¼, 8½, 10½, 3½
St. John the Evangelist. 13th. ab. Chestnut, 6½, 8, 10½ 4
St. Josephs, Willings al., 6, 7, 8½, 10½ a. m., 5½ p. m.
St. Malachy, 11th, ab. Master, 6, 7, 9, 10½ a. m., 3½ p. m.
St. Mary, 4th, ab. Spruce, 6, 8½, 10½ a. m., 3½ p. m.
St. Mary Magdalene di Pazzi, Merriott, ab. 7th, 8, 10 3½
St. Michael, 2d, ab. Master, 6, 7, 8, 9, 10½ a. m., 3½ p. m.
St. Patrick, 20th ab. Spruce, 6, 7, 8, 9, 10½ a. m., 3½ p. m.
St. Paul, Christian, ab. 9th, 6, 7½, 8, 9, 10½ a. m., 3½ p. m.
St. Peter, 5th & Girard av., 5½, 6½, 7½, 8½, 10 a. m., 2¾, 7 p.m.
St. Philips de Neri, Queen, ab. 2d, 6, 8, 9, 10¼ a. m., 3½ p. m.
St. Stephens, Nicetown, 7½, 10½ a. m., 3½ p. m.
St. Teresa, Broad & Catherine
St. Veronica, 2d & Butler, 8, 10½ a. m., 3 p. m.
St. Vincent de Paul, Price and Evans, 6, 8, 9¼, 10½ 4
St. Vincent, Tacony, 10½, 3

SPIRITUAL ASSOCIATIONS.
Co-Operative, 240 S. 5th
First, 810 Spring Garden
Keystone, 8th & Spring Garden
Second, Thompson, 1 el. Fror¹

UNITARIAN.
Broad & Spring Garden
First, 10th and Locust
Germantown, Green & Chelton av.

UNITED BRETHREN.
First, 4th, ab. Norris
Second, Edgemont & Westmoreland

UNITED PRESBYTERIAN.
Eighth, Bainbridge, ab. 11th
Fifth, 20th & Buttonwood
First, Broad and Lombard
Fourth, 19th and Fitzwater
Norris sq., Susquehanna av. & Hancock
North, Master, ab. 15th
Second, Race, ab. 15th
Seventh, Orthodox & Leiper, (Fkd.)
Tenth, 88th and Hamilton

UNIVERSALIST.
All Souls, Broad & Spring Garden
Church of the Messiah, Locust, ab. 13th
Church of the Restoration, Master, ab. 16th

# AMUSEMENTS.

Academy of Music, Broad and Locust
Academy of Fine Arts, Broad and Cherry, (every other Sunday Free.)
Arch St. Opera House, Arch St. ab. 10th
Arch St. Theater, Arch, ab. 6th
Eleventh St. Opera House, 11th ab. Chestnut
Franklin Institute, (Monthly Free Lectures), 7th, ab. Chestnut
Haverly's Theater, Chestnut, ab. 12th
Horticultural Hall, (Free), West Park
Lyceum, Broad ab. Spruce
National Museum, (Free), Independence Hall
Opera House, Chestnut ab. 10th
Pennsylvania Museum, (Free), Memorial Hall, West Park
Wagner Institute, (Free Lecture) Montgomery av.
Walnut St. Theater, 9th and Walnut
Zoological Garden, West Park

## ZOOLOGICAL GARDEN DIRECTORY.

Beautifully and conveniently located, (accessible by the steamboats which ply at frequent intervals up and down the Schuylkill, and the street cars from all parts of the city,) on the west side of the Schuylkill, just below the Girard av. bridge, in that part of the park known as ' Solitude,'' is the ZOOLOGICAL GARDEN. As we enter by the Gothic structure or gate, on the north end, a little to the right, is

THE CARNIVORA HOUSE, the home of the lions, giraffes, tigers, kangaroos, hyenas, leopards, etc. Just south of the Carnivora House is

THE MONKEY HOUSE, which every one seems desirous of seeing. Out of the Monkey House, by the western door, the road leads us to

THE AVIARY, which contains many rare and beautiful birds from all parts of the world.

THE FOX PENS are west of the Aviary, and adjoin

THE WOLF PENS; and on the same road is

THE RACCOON HOUSE, Directly opposite the Aviary is

THE PRAIRIE-DOG VILLAGE, after admiring which, we go to

THE ELEPHANT HOUSE and see the elephants, then take a look at the

RHINOCEROS and the Guinea Pigs; not neglecting

THE RABBIT HOUSE, on the way to

THE EAGLE AVIARY, where will be found several fine specimens of these interesting birds; after which we pay a visit to

THE DEER ENCLOSURE, then on to

THE BISON SHEDS, and take a look at the Buffalo; then last though not least in attractiveness are

THE BEAR PITS, which will be found on the eastern side of the Garden on the river walk.

There are many other objects of interest here which must be seen to be appreciated.

# CITY RAILWAY DIRECTORY.

The following is the running direction of the city railway cars. It frequently occurs that persons unfamiliar with the routes get on cars that traverse but a short distance on the streets of other lines, they are cautioned not to pay their fare unless certain the car goes the proper distance, to prevent such mistakes, state your destination to the conductor when paying fare.

On several lines transfer tickets to other branches are given, whilst others charge extra on same line and further distance; information relative to this may be obtained of the conductors.

Transfer or exchange tickets can be had to Fairmount Park from most of the lines running north or west, when not running direct to the Park.

Those lines running direct to the Park are designated thus *

### CARS RUNNING NORTH.

Front St., *Chestnut to Vine, Thompson to Amber.
Howard, fr. Columbia av. to Huntingdon.
Frankford av. Oxford to Frankford.
3d, Mifflin to Oxford.
5th, Jackson to Lehigh av.
7th, *Spring Garden to Susquehanna av.
Germantown av to Gtn.
8th, Dickinson to Columbia av
9th, *McKean to Spg. Gard'n;
Ridge av. *9th to Manayunk.
10th, Diamond to Germantown av.
11th, Reed to Susquehanna av.
Broad, Columbia av. to Somerset.
15th, Carpenter to Norris
16th, Carpenter to Susquehanna av.
18th, Sansom to Montgomery av
19th, Carpenter to Norris.
21st, *Arch to Callowhill.
23d, *Spruce to Green
33d, fr. *Spruce to Eadline.
35th, *fr. Spring Garpen to Zoological Garden.
38th, *fr. Spruce to Lancaster av.
41st,*fr. Market to Elm av.

### CARS RUNNING EAST.

Dickinson, *fr. 12th to 8th.
Federal, fr. 7th to Front.
Christian, fr. 23d to 5th.
Lombard, fr. 25th to Front.
Spruce, fr. 36th to 3d.
Chestnut, fr. 42d to Front.
Market, fr. 65th to Front,
Baring, fr. 41st to 33d.
Filbert, fr. 20th to 7th.
Arch, fr .20th to 2d.
Race, fr. 22d to 2d.
Callowhill, fr. 26th to Front.
Spring Garden 25th to 7th.
Green, fr. 25th to Beach.
Wallace, fr. 23d to Franklin.
Girard Avenue, fr. Belmont av. to Palmer.
Thompson, fr. Franklin to Front.
Jffersn, fr. 27th to Franklin.
Columbia av.fr. 35th to Howard
Berks, fr. 5th to Front.
Lehigh av. fr. 5th to Kensington av.

### CARS RUNNING SOUTH.

Front, fr. Callowhill to Chestnut and fr. Dock to Lombard
Hancock, fr. Huntingdon to Susquehanna av.
Frankford av., fr. Frankford to Jefferson st.

4th, fr. Germantown av. to Dickinson.
6th, fr. Lehigh av. to Jackson.
7th, fr. Race to Federal.
Franklin, fr. Susquehanna av. to Race.
Ridge av. fr. Manayunk to 10th
10th, fr. Diamond to Mifflin.
12th, Susquehanna av. to Wharton, & fr. Mifflin to Snyder av.
13th, fr. Somerset to McKean.
17th, fr. Norris to Carpenter.
18th, fr. Filbert to Wharton.
20th, fr. Montgomery av to Filbert,
22d, fr. Wallace to Filbert.
35th, fr. Zoological Garden to Powelton ave.
40th, fr. Elm av. to Baltimore av
Germantown, fr. Gtn av. to 7th
Pasyunk av. fr. South to Snyder av.
CARS RUNNING WEST.
Snyder av. fr. 12th to Broad.
Ellsworth, fr. 8th to 23d.

Wharton, fr. 12th to 17th. and fr. Front to 9th.
South, fr. Front to 27th.
Pine, *fr. 2d to 23d.
Sansom, fr. 6th to 18th.
Walnut, *fr. Front to 22d.
Chestnut, *fr. 22d to 41st.
Market, *fr. Front to 65th.
Arch, *fr. 2d to 21st.
Vine, *fr. 3d to 23d.
Callowhll, *fr. Front to 26th.
Spring Garden, *fr. 9th to 23d.
Fairmount av *fr Delaware av to 25th.
Poplar, *fr. 7th to 29th.
Girard av. *fr. Palmer to Belmont av.
Lancaster av. *fr. 32d to 52.
Richmond, fr. Bridge to Frankford av.
Master, fr. *Frankf'd av to 27th
Columbia av *fr. Front to 34th
Berks, fr. Front to 6th.
Spruce, *fr. 30th to 38th.
Lehigh av. fr. Kensington av. to 6th

## TELEGRAPH COMPANIES.

**AMERICAN DISTRICT.**
3d and Chestnut
8th and Chestnut
Broad and Chestnut
20th and Locust
40th and Locust
36th and Lancaster av
Broad and Wood
8th and Wood
20th and Callowhill
Jefferson and Carlisle
**AMERICAN RAPID.**
Chestnut, ab. 3d
**AMERICAN UNION.**
102 South 3d

**CONTINENTAL.**
235 Chestnut
**GOLD & STOCK.**
3d and Chestnut
**MUTUAL UNION.**
103 Walnut
**PHILADELPHIA LOCAL.**
10th and Chestnut
**PHILADELPHIA & READING.**
204 South 4th
**POLICE & FIRE ALARM.**
5th and Chestnut

## HOTELS.

American, Chestnut, ab. 5th
Aldine, Chestnut, ab. 19th
Allegheny, Market, ab. 8th
Bellevue, Broad and Walnut
Bingham, 11th and Market
Colonnade, 15th and Chestnut
Continental, 9th and Chestnut
Commercial, Market ab. 8th
Girard, 9th and Chestnut
Guy's, 7th and Chestnut

Lafayette, Broad and Chestnut
Merchant's, 4th ab. Market
Ridgway, Delaware av. & Market
St. Charles, 3d and Arch
St. Cloud, Arch, ab. 7th
St. Elmo, Arch ab. 3d
St. George, Broad and Walnut
Washington, Chestnut, ab. 7th
West End, Chestnut, ab. 15th

# STEAM RAILWAYS.

**BERK STREET DEPOT.**
(American and Berks.)
Bound Brook R. R.
N. Penna. R. R.
Lehigh Valley R. R.
Philadelphia & Reading R. R.

**BROAD STREET STATION**
Baltimore and Ohio R. R.
Baltimore and Potomac R. R.
Belvidere R. R.
Cumberland Valley R. R.
Del. Lack. & Western R. R.
Northern Central R. R.
Pennsylvania Central R. R.
Phila., Wil. and Balt. R. R.
Shenandoah Valley R. R.
W. Chester & Philadelphia R. R.
Wilmington & Northern R. R.

Virginia Midland R. R.
**CALLOWHILL STREET DEPOT.**
Catawissa R. R. Callowhill and 13th
Philadelphia & Reading R. R.
**FOOT OF MARKET STREET.**
Cam. and Amboy Div. P. R. R.
West Jersey R. R.
**FOOT OF SOUTH STREET.**
Cam., Glouces & Mt. Eph. R. R.
**FOOT OF VINE.**
Camden and Atlantic R. R.
**KENSINGTON DEPOT.**
(Front and Berks.)
Pennsylvania Central R. R.
**PIER 8 S. Wharves.**
(Delaware av. ab. Walnut.)
Philadelphia & Atlantic R. R.

# FERRIES.

**CAMDEN.**
Fr. South St. to Kaign's Point
**CAMDEN & PHILADEPHIA.**
**COOPERS POINT.**
Fr. Vine St. & Shackamaxon St. to Cooper's Pt.

**GLOUCESTER.**
Fr. South St.
**WEST JERSEY.**
Fr. Market to Market St. Camden

THE CENTRAL HIGH SCHOOL.

# THE NEW STREET DIRECTORY OF PHILADELPHIA.

## Showing the Streets, Avenues, Lanes, Courts, Places, Etc.

### EXPLANATION.

☞ The Streets running North and South, across the City, are from 2d to 72d in numerical order. Divided by Market they are called North and South; those above Market being called North, and those below Market South.

The decimal system of numbering the houses being used, 100 is allowed for each square North and South of Market, and West from the Delaware river: thus No. 200 North Third street would be at Race, 200 South Third at Walnut, 200 Walnut at Second, and 300 at Third, and so on. The even numbers are on the South and West sides, and the odd numbers on the North and East sides.

## TABLE OF THE NUMBERS OF THE MAIN STREETS RUNNING EAST AND WEST.

### North of Market.

| | | |
|---|---|---|
| 100 Arch. | 2100 Diamond. | 4000 Luzerne. |
| 200 Race. | 2200 Susquehanna. | 4100 Roxborough. |
| 300 Vine. | 2300 Dauphin. | 4200 Juniata. |
| 400 Callowhill. | 2400 York. | 4300 Bristol. |
| 500 Noble. | 2500 Cumberland. | 4400 Cayuga. |
| 600 Green. | 2600 Huntingdon. | 4500 Wingohocking. |
| 700 Fairmount av. | 2700 Lehigh Av. | 4600 Courtland. |
| 800 Brown. | 2800 Somerset. | 4700 Wyalusing. |
| 900 Poplar. | 2900 Cambria. | 4800 Wyoming. |
| 1000 Otter. | 3000 Indiana. | 4900 London. |
| 1100 George. | 3100 Clearfield. | 5000 Rockland. |
| 1200 Girard Av. | 3200 Allegheny. | 5100 Ruscomb. |
| 1300 Thompson. | 3300 Westmoreland | 5200 Lindley. |
| 1400 Master. | 3400 Ontario. | 5300 Wisteria. |
| 1500 Jefferson. | 3500 Tioga. | 5400 Fisher. |
| 1600 Oxford. | 3600 Venango | 5500 Somerville. |
| 1700 Columbia Av. | 3700 Erie. | 5600 Clarkson. |
| 1800 Montgomery. | 3800 Butler. | 5700 Olney. |
| 1900 Berks. | 3900 Pike. | 5800 Chew. |
| 2000 Norris. | | |

### South of Market.

| | | |
|---|---|---|
| 100 Chestnut. | 1600 Tasker. | 3100 Packer. |
| 200 Walnut. | 1700 Morris. | 3200 Curtin. |
| 300 Spruce. | 1800 Moore. | 3300 Geary. |
| 400 Pine. | 1900 Mifflin. | 3400 Hartranft. |
| 500 Lombard. | 2000 McKean. | 3500 Hoyt. |
| 600 South. | 2100 Snyder. | 3600 36th Av. |
| 700 Bainbridge. | 2200 Jackson. | 3700 37th Av. |
| 800 Catherine. | 2300 Wolf. | 3800 38th Av. |
| 900 Christian. | 2400 Ritner. | 3900 39th Av. |
| 1000 Carpenter. | 2500 Porter. | 4000 40th Av. |
| 1100 Washington Av. | 2600 Shunk. | 4100 41st Av. |
| 1200 Federal. | 2700 Oregon. | 4200 42d Av. |
| 1300 Wharton. | 2800 Johnston. | 4300 43d Av. |
| 1400 Reed. | 2900 Bigler. | 4400 44th Av. |
| 1500 Dickerson. | 3000 Pollock. | 4500 45th Av. |

# NEW STREET DIRECTORY.

## ABBREVIATIONS.

| | | | | | |
|---|---|---|---|---|---|
| ab. | Above, North or West of | C. H. | Chestnut Hill | Myk. | Manyunk |
| al. | Alley | c. | Corner | N. | North |
| av. | Avenue | cr. | Creek | pk. | Park |
| bel. | Below, East or South of | ct. | Court | pl. | Place |
| | | E. | East | rd. | Road |
| | | Fkd. | Frankford | S. | South |
| bet. | Between | fr. | From | sqr. | Square |
| Bdg. | Bridesburg | Gtn. | Germantown | W. | West |

A., W. fr. 22d, ab. Thompson
A., N. fr. 2500 Kensington av
Abbott's ct., fr. 529 Fitzwater
Abel pl., fr. 1021 Lemon
Aberdeen, fr., 214 Spruce
Abigail, W. fr. Amber, bel. Otis
Abbottsford, fr. 3215 N. 36th
Academy, W fr. 10th, ab. Arch
Accomac pl., fr. 311 Wildey
Acorn al., fr. Locust, ab. 8th
Acton pl S. fr. Pearl, ab. 11th
Adair av., fr. 415 N. 13th
Adaline, fr. Margaret (Fkd.)
Adams, fr. Frankford, (Fkd)
Adams, fr. 2422 Commerce
Adams, fr. Walnut la. (Gtn.)
Addison, W. fr. 17th, bel. Pine
Adelphia, W. fr. 214 S. 5th
Adelphia, al., fr. 152 Pegg
Adrain, E. fr. Ridge av. (Myk.)
Adrain, N. fr. 45 Otter
Alton, W. fr. 1126 S. 16th
Agate. N. fr. Ann, bel Tulip
Agnes, S. fr. Christian, ab. 10th
Airy, N. fr. Thompson, ab. 13th
Alaska, fr. 618 Passyunk av
Albergen ct., fr. Willow, ab. 7th
Albert, fr. 1028 S. 12th
Albert, W.fr. Emerald,bel. Ann
Albert av., fr. 1220 Palmer
Alberto av., fr. 1210 Palmer
Albion, S. fr. Pine, ab. 21st
Albion, N. fr. Arch, ab. 21st
Albion, N. fr. Spruce, ab. 21st
Alder, N. fr. Poplar, ab. 16th
Alexander, fr. 624 Fitzwater
Alexander, fr. 1523 Wharton
Alfred, fr. Queen, (Gtn.)
Alford, E. fr. 6th, bel. Pine

Alice ct., fr. 1013 Sansom
Allens la., S. fr. Gtn. av. (Gtn.)
Allens ct., fr. 925 Rodman
Allegheny av., E. & W., 3200 N.
Allen, S. W. fr. Mary to 41st
Allen, S. fr. Palmer, ab Beach
Allen, W. fr. Frankford, (Fkd.)
Allen la., fr. Gtn.av. (Gtn.)
Allen's ct., fr. 720 Bainbridge
Allen's ct., fr. 613 Minster
Allison, S. fr. Arch, ab. 56th
Allison pl., fr. 120 N. Front
Almendo, fr. 1029 Cumberland
Almira, pl. fr. 722 N. Front
Almond, E. fr. 719 S. 2d,
Almond. fr. Ash (Bdg.)
Almont pl., fr. 1529 Cadwalader
Alroy, W. fr. Ridge av., ab. 13th
Alter, fr. 1118 S. 17th
Alton ct., S. fr. Richard ab. 16th
Aman, fr. 1421 S. 12th
Amanda pl. fr. 2319 Pearl
Amber, N. E. fr. Front & Norris
Ambler's ct. fr. 1319 Heath
Amboy, fr. 1321 Jefferson
Amelia, W. fr. 5th ab. Mifflin
America, fr. Byron, bel. Myrtle
American, N. fr. Master, ab. 2d
American W. fr. 23 ab. Hare
American pl., fr. 221 N. 4th
Americus, S. fr. Oxen, ab. 8th
Amity, fr. 1421 Stiles ab. 14th
Amos pa., fr. 1521 Randolph
Anadale pl., fr. 723 N. 9th
Analine, S. fr. Federal, ab. 17th
Annapolis, S. fr. South, bel. 2d
Anderson, S.fr.Indiana ab.1 th
Andress, S. fr. Mellon, ab. 12th
Anger, N. fr. Race, ab. 33d

Anita, fr. 1120 S. 10th
Ann, E. fr. Amber & Indiana
Ann, W. fr. 17th, ab. Spruce
Ann, W. fr. Trenton av. (Fkd.)
Ann, W. fr. 2634 Emerald
Ann pl., E. fr, 1319 Wheat
Anthony, fr. 722 Dickerson
Anthracite, fr. 2631 Belgrade
Apple, W. fr. 1328 Wheat
Apple,S.fr.Lancaster av.ab.50th
Apple, W. fr. Cedar, (Myk.)
Appletree al., fr. 226 N. 4th
Apsley, S. fr.Gtn,av.ab.Berkley
Arabella, fr.522 Washington av
Aramingo, fr. 2420 Commerce
Aramingo, W. fr. Paul, (Fkd.)
Arazonia, fr. 2320 N. 9th
Arch, E. & W., 200 N.
Arch av. fr. 517 Dillwyn
Archibold pl. fr. 1318 Race
Arlington, fr. 1928 N. 17th
Arizona, W. fr. 12th ab. Spruce
Armand pl., fr. 720 Marshall
Armat, N. fr. Gtn. av. (Gtn.)
Armstrong ct., fr. 419 Locust
Armstrong ct.,fr.1218 Catherine
Arrison, fr. 126 S. 15th
Arrott, E. fr. Oakland, (Fkd.)
Artisan, S. fr. Ball, (Bdg.)
Ash, W. fr. Richmond,ab. York
Ashburton, W. fr. 23d, bel. Pine
Ashbury, S. fr. South, ab. 5th
Ashhurst, S. fr. Market, ab. 2d
Ashhole, Spruce, ab. 33d
Ashland, N. fr. Wharton,ab.10th
Ashland, E. fr. Stiles, (Fkd.)
Ashland, E. fr. Penn, (Myk.)
Ashmead, S. fr. Clinton, (Gtn.)
Ashton pl., E. fr. 23d ab. Race
Aspen, W. from 500 N. 35th
Aspen, Spruce, ab. 21st
Aspen St. pl., fr. 415 Albion
Astor pl., N. Front, ab. Brown
Asylum, E. fr. 15th, bel. Spruce
Asylum, S. fr. 1412 Spruce
Asylum rd., N.fr.Adams,(Fkd.)
Atherton, S. fr. Marriott, ab. 5th
Atkinson ct., N. fr. 529 Lombard
Atlanta, W. fr. 17th ab. Tioga
Atlantic, E., fr. York ab.16th
Atlee pl. fr. 728 Humes av
Almore, W. fr. 13th, ab. Brown
Atwood pl., fr. 1020 Hamilton
Auburn fr. 1030 S. 8th
Auburn, W. fr. Trenton, (Fkd.)
Audubon pl., fr. 28 N. 4th
Augusta pl.W.fr.Front,ab.Race
Aurora, W. fr. 9th, ab. Spruce
Austin, S. fr. Federal, ab. 10th
Austin, pl. fr. 831 St. John,
Autumn, S. fr. Barker, ab. 19th
Autumn, S. fr. Vine, ab. 17th
Avenue C.,E.fr.323 New Market

Avon pl., E. fr. 433 N. 13th
Award's ct., W. fr. 328 Dugan
Aydellotte ct., N. fr. Parham
Azalia, E. fr. 15th, ab. Race
B, W. fr. 23d, bel. Master
B., N. fr. Kensington av. ab A
Bache ct., fr. 1423 Race,
Baden, S. fr. Alaska, ab, 7th
Bailey, N. fr. Jefferson, ab. 26th
Bailey's ct., N. fr. John, bel. 2d
Bailey's ct., W. fr. 1226 Mascher
Bainbridge. E. & W., 700 S.
Baird, W. fr. Queen, (Gtn.)
Baird's av., N. fr. 1323 Brown
Baker's al., fr. 515 Powell
Baker's ct., fr. 941 Alder
Baker pl., W. from 320 St. John
Baker, E. fr. 8th ab. Catherine
Baker, E., fr. Gtn. av., (Gtn.)
Baker, fr. Green la. (Myk.)
Baldwin, pl. fr. 529 York.
Ball, fr. 2021 Richmond
Ballenger av. fr. 1020 Race
Ball's ct., fr. Front, ab. Poplar
Balsam pl., fr. 747 S. 5th
Balston pl., N.fr.Concord,ab. 2d
Baltic pl., N.fr.Catharine, ab. 2d
Baltimore av. S. W. fr. 39th &
   Woodland av
Baltz, S. fr. Thompson, ab. 30th
Bambrey, S. fr. Poplar, ab. 25th
Banana,W.fr.15th,ab.Girard av
Bancroft, S.fr.Wharton,ab.16th
Bangor, fr. 730 Lloyd
Bank, S. fr. Market, bel. 3d
Banker's av.,fr.Warren, ab.39th
Bankson, N.fr.Wallace, ab. 13th
Barbary pl., E. fr. Vaughan
Barber's row, fr. 1129 Mellon
Barclay, fr. 640 N. Broad
Barcroft, N.fr.McKean, ab. 10th
Baring, W. fr. 32d ab. Race
Barker, fr. 18 S. 16th
Barker's ct., W. fr. Crease
Barley, W. fr. 10th, bel. Pine
Barley-Corn, Alaska, ab. 4th
Barlow pl., N. fr. Baker, ab. 7th
Barlow, S. fr. Wharton, bel. 5th
Barnes' pl., fr. 1123 Charlotte
Barnet, W. fr. 1118 S. 8th
Barnewell, S. fr. Pine, ab. 25th
Barney av., fr. 2217 Shamokin
Barnhurst pl., fr. 1825 Francis
Barron, S. fr. Gaskill, ab. 2d
Barrow, S. fr. South, ab. 3d
Bartholomew ct., fr. 918 S. 5th
Barton, N. fr. Wallace, ab. 10th
Bartram, N.fr.Jefferson, ab.20th
Bartram, fr. 318 S. 6th
Bascom pl., N. fr. 1033 Barley
Bastion pl., fr. 418 German
Bass, E. fr. Pleasant, (Gtn.)
Bath, N. fr. William, ab. 12th

THE NEW MASONIC TEMPLE,
Cor. Broad and Filbert Sts.

Bateman, N. fr. Reed, ab. 19th
Baton, S. fr. McKean, ab. 20th
Baursach's ct., fr. 1330 N. Front
Baxter pl., fr. 708 Marshall
Bay, W. fr. 6th, bel. Spruce
Bayard, W. fr. 7th, ab. Catharine
Baynon pl., fr. 960 Marshall
Baytree pl., fr. Pine, ab. 6th
Baynton, E. fr. Wister, (Gtn.)
Beach, N. fr. Willow, bel. Front
Beale pl., fr. 1720 St. Joseph's av
Bean pl., N. fr. Race, above 2d
Beard ct., W. fr. 5th, ab. Jefferson
Beaumont p'., N. fr. Pegg
Beaver, W. fr. 2d, ab. Poplar
Beaver, S. Tasker, bel. Ash
Beck, fr. 817 N Front
Beck pl. fr. 824 S. Front
Beckel av., fr. 532 Linden
Becker pl., fr. 318 St. John
Becker, fr. 634 N. 16th
Becket's ct, fr. 930 S. Front
Beckett, W. fr. Hamilton Ter.
Beckman's ct., E. fr. 717 St. John
Beck's pl., S. fr. Christian, ab. 2d
Beckwith, fr. 11.7 Catharine
Beckman pl., fr. 429 Green.
Bedloe pl., fr. 1321 Carlton
Beeler's ct., fr. 835 Charlotte
Beech av., E. fr. 24th, ab. Locust
Beechwood, N. fr. Columbia av ab. 21st
Bela r, W. fr. Mechanic, (Myk.
Belden's row, N. fr. Shellbark,
Belfast pl., fr. 43 Beck
Belgrade, fr. 1431 Frankford av.
Belgrade pl., fr. 1119 Columbia
Belinda pl. N. fr. Alaska, ab. 7th
Bell, N. fr. Market, ab. 40th
Bell's ct., S. fr. Ohio, ab. 11th
Bellevue, N. fr. Francis, ab. 17th
Bellevue, W. fr. 20th, bel. Ontario
Belmont av., N. fr. Lancaster av. & 44th
Belrose, N. fr. Willow. ab. 2d
Belrose ct., S. fr. 1244 Catharine
Benedict pl., fr. 1015 Hamilton
Benezet, E. fr. 11th, ab. Market
Benfer's ct., fr. 1031 St. John
Bennett, W. fr. 7th, bel. Chestnut
Bennett ct, N. fr. Cherry, ab. 3d
Benner lle, pl. fr. 724 lisle
Bentley s ct, fr. 86 N. 4th
Benton, S. fr. Market, ab. 15th
Bell's ct., ab. Spruce
Berks, E. & W. 1900 N.
Ber in, S. fr. Gaskill ab. 4th
Bergess, fr. 2031 Amber
Ferlin, S fr. Gaskill, ab. 4th
Bermuda, fr. Tucker, (Fkd.)
Bernard s ct., fr. 776 S. 2d
Berry l., S. fr. Locust, ab. 9th
Berkley, S. fr. Straw

Berry's av., fr. 1371 Charlotte
Berry, W. fr. 262 N. 41st
Bertrand pl., fr. 1248 Cadwalader
Bethlehem, fr. 121 E. Venango,
Beulah, S. fr, Tasker, ab. 7th
Bevan's av., fr. 213 Washgt., av
Beverly pl., fr. 827 Bainbridge
Bevin, S. W. fr. Reading, av.
Bickam's ct., fr. 620 S. Front
Bicking, fr. 6122 Wood and av
Biddle, fr. 27 N. 25th
Bigler, E. & W. 2900 S.
Billington, fr. 9 S 9th
Binder's ct., S. fr. Poplar. ab. 9th
Bingham pl., E. fr. 3 bel. Baring
Bixly, S. fr. Pulaski, (Gtn.,)
Bingham's ct., fr. 317 Spruce
Birch, S. fr. Fitzwater, ab. 1th
Birch, N. W. fr. Salmon, bel. Ann
Birch pl., W. fr. 8th, ab. Arch
Bishop, fr. 649 Richmond
Black Horse al., fr. 23 S. 2d
Blackburn, N. fr. Mifflin. ab. 10th
Bladen ct., N. fr. E freth al
Blair, N. fr. Norris bel. Front
Blake pl., fr. 877 Lawrence
Blake's ct., S. fr. South, ab. 8th
Blanche, S. fr. 936 Marshall
Blight, N. fr. Lombard ab. 13th
Blighton, 216 S. Broad
Blight, fr. 1321 Lombard
Blinn's ct. W. fr. 4th, ab. Brown
Bliss, W. fr. Rasberry
Block pl., 1724 Richmond
Blodgett, N. fr. Centre, ab. 37th
Blunston av., 31 S. 19th
Bodine, N. f", Jefferson, ab. 2d
Bohemia pl., E. fr. 767 S. 4th
Bolivar pl., W. fr. 2d ab. Vine
Bolivia pl., E. f. 11th, ab. Race
Bolton, E. fr. Bath. bel. Tioga
Bolton, E. fr. 23d ab. Jefferson
Bond, W. fr. 9 bel. Spruce
Bonner pl., N. f. Laurel, bel. 2d
Boone, fr. 1416 Lancaster
Bordon, fr. 13.1 S. 5th
Bosler, 'r. 215 N 11th
Boudino' S, fr. Indiana ab. B
Bounty, N. f. Federal, ab. 16th
Bouvier al., N. fr. 121 Walnut
Bouvier, N. fr. Master, ab. 17th
Bowen pl., fr. 910 S. 17th
Bower, fr. 1929 Frankford av
Bower pl., fr. 818 Rachel
Bowery pl., fr. 36 Dugan,
Bowery pl., W. fr 408 Canton
Bowers pl., fr. 1715 Perkiomen
Bowman, N. E fr. 36 bel. Queen
Bowser, W. fr. Mulberry, (Fkd.)
Boyd's av, fr. 1021 Morgan
Boyer pl. fr. 29 S. 10th
Boyer, W. fr. Church la. (Gtn.)

INDEPENDENCE HALL, 1776.

Boyle ct. N. fr. Filbert, ab. 6th
Boyd's ct., N. fr. Chant ct
Brabant.N. fr.William bel. Bath
Bracelandt's ct., fr. 916 S. Front
Braddock, fr. 335 Huntingdon
Bradford, S. fr. Spruce, ab. 16th
Bradford av., fr. 729 St. Mary
Bramble, pl., fr. 747 Passayunk av
Branchtown Pike, fr. Boyer, (Gtn.)
Branch, W. fr. 3d, ab. Race
Brandywine. W. fr. 528 N. 13th
Brannen al., S. fr. Vine, ab. 5th
Bread, N. fr. Arch, ab. 2d
Breese, w. fr. Prosperous al
Bremau pl., fr. Cadwalader
Brewery pl., fr. 722 S. Juniper
Bride pl., N. fr. 1223 Hamilton
Bridge, fr. Frankford av. (Fkd.)
Brier, pl., N. fr. Spruce, ab. 10th
Brighton, E fr. 15th, ab. Spruce
Briggs, E. fr. 231 Madison
Bright, N. fr. William, ab. Tulip
Brilling's ct., N. fr. Union, ab. 2d
Bringburst, N fr. Gtn. av. (Gtn)
Brinkley pl., S.fr.Cherry,ab.6th
Brinton, E.fr.13th,ab Catharine
Brinton, S. fr. Oxford, ab. 4th
Brighton, E. fr. 922 S. 8th
Bristol, E. & W. 4300 N.
Bristol av. E.fr Front.ab.Laurel
Bristol pl.. fr. 615 Guilford
Bristow pl., W. fr. Tamerind
Broad, N. & S., ab. 13th
Broad, N. fr. Levering, (Myk.)
Brodie pl., fr. 951 St. John
Brogan, W. fr. Raspberry
Bromley pl., S. fr. Brown, ab. 2d
Brown's ct., fr. 406 N. 23d
Brown, N. fr. Buckius, (Bdg.)
Brown, E. & W. 800 N.
Brown's ct., fr. 1013 Helmuth
Brown's ct., fr. Monroe, ab. 4th
Brown's ct., fr. 804 Perkiomen
Brown's ct., fr. 735 St. Mary
Brown's ct., fr. 722 South
Browker, fr. Hedge, (Fkd.)
Brunswick pl., fr. 327 Stanley
Brussel's pl.,W.fr.5th, bel.Green
Buchanan pl., fr. 431 N. 23d
Buchanan pl., fr. Aberdeen
Buck rd., N.W. fr. 2000 Reed
Buckingham pl., fr. 221 Poplar
Buckley, W. fr. 5th, bel. Spruce
Bucknell, N. fr. Hare, ab. 23d
Buck's ct., fr. 819 Catharine
Buck's ct.,W.fr.11th, bel. Spruce
Bockius, fr. Frankford cr.(Bdg)
Bucknell, N. fr. Hare, ab. 23d
Budd, fr. 4034 Baring
Budd, W. fr. 12th, ab. Pine
Buddin's ct., N. fr. Buddin's al.
Buddin's al., W. fr. 12th,ab.Arch
Buist's c ., fr. 1214 Fitzwater
Bulletin, E. fr. 843 S. Front
Bummerscheim ct.,fr.1714 N.8th
Bunting av., fr. Marston
Bunyan pl., fr. 1305 Lancaster
Burbank pl., fr. Vincent
Burbridge,W. fr. Norton, (Gtn.)
Burchell's ct., fr. 835 S. 3rd
Burd, N. fr. Green, bel. 2d
Burges's pl., fr. 322 Columbia
Burgundy pl., fr. 830 N. 8th
Burlington pl., fr. 235 German
Burnett, S. fr.Christian, ab. 25th.
Burns, fr. 1421 Brown
Burrow's ct., S. fr. Minster
Burr's av., fr. 1415 Wood
Burton, W. fr. 15th, ab. South
Burwick pl., fr.725 New Market
Butcher,W.fr. Rose, bel. Market
Butler, E. & W. 3800 N.
Butler av., W. fr. 13 6 Pine
Butler pl., S.fr. Sansom, ab. 10th
Button, fr. 18 N. 13. h
Buttonwood,W.fr..d, ab. Noble
Butz, N. fr. Noble, ab. 2d
Butz row, fr. 491 St. John.
Byron, fr. 3135 Richmond
Byron pl., E. fr. Gtn. av., ab. 3d
C, N fr. Kensingtou av., ab. B,.
Cabin, fr. 1913 Pennsylvania av
Cabot, fr. 12.4 N. 15th
Cabot, N. E, fr. Anthracite
Cadbury av., N. fr. Jefferson
Cadwalader, fr. 141 Girard av.
Cadwalader ct., 1417 Fitzwater
Cahawha pl., fr. 418 S. 12th
Cahill pl., fr. 422 N. Front
Caldwell, fr. 207 S. 24th
Caldwel,W. fr. 13th, ab. Poplar
Caledonia av., fr. 1021 Filbert
California pl.. fr. 1117 Rodman
Callowhill, E. & W. 40 J N
Calvert pl., fr. 1718 Vesey
Calvert, fr. Metcalf
Calvin pl , fr. 829 N. 7th
Camac, N. fr. Master, ab. 12th
Camac, E. fr. 1621 Lawrence
Cambria, E. & W. 2900 N.
Cambridge, fr. 925 Carlisle
Camoridge, fr. Tucker, (Fkd.)
Camelia, S. fr, Deal
Cameron, fr. 816 Francis
Cameron pl., fr. 1420 N. 4th.
Cameronian ct., S. fr. Marble
Camilla, fr. 1011 S. 11th
Camp pl., S. fr. Brown, ab. 4th
Campbell, fr. 522 Fitzwater
Canal, fr. 2620 Walker
Canal, fr. 1034 Frankford av
Canal, E. fr 5th, ab. Mifflin
Canby, W. fr. 12th. bel. Walnut
Candia pl., fr. 516 Fairmount av

Candy row, fr. 108 S. 24th
Cane's ct., W. fr. 7th, ab. South
Canover, N. fr. Vine, ab. 57th
Canning pl., fr. 929 Willow
Cantman pl., fr. 678 N. 11th
Canton, fr. 917 Callowhill
Cantrell, fr. 1918 S. 9th.
Cantrell ct., fr. 1028 S. 2d
Cantwell pl., for 319 Cherry
Capewell,W.fr.Belgrade,ab Otis
Capital, fr. 2020 Parrish
Carath pl., fr. 412 Wharton
Carberry ct., fr. 420 Catharine
Carbon, S. fr. South, ab. 10th
Carbon ct., fr. 517 Marriott
Carbon, fr. Ontario, ab. Del. av.
Carlisle, N. fr. 1421 Brown
Carlton, W. fr. 10th, ab. Wood
Carman pl., fr. 717 Arch
Carney av., fr. 225 S. Juniper
Carolery, W. fr. 5th, ab. Vine
Caroline pl., fr. 1014 Barley
Caroline, fr. 429 Wharton
Carpenter, E. & W. 1000 S,
Carpenter,fr.5464Gtn.av.,(Gtn.)
Carpenter's ct., fr. 330 Chestnut
Carpenter la.,S.fr.Gtn. av.,(Gtn)
Carric, fr. Garden, (Bdg.)
Carroll pl., Front ab. Adrian
Carroll ct., fr. 1528 Lombard
Carr's ct., fr. 830 Catharine
Carsell av., fr. 717 N. Broad
Carswell pl., fr. 1109 Charles.
Carters, W. fr. 2d, bel. Chestnut
Carver, W. fr. 15th, ab. South
Cascon pl., fr. 332 New Market
Caseltine av.,S.fr.Wood,ab.20th
Casper av., S. fr. Jones, ab. 17th
Casper, S. fr.Erie av.,ab.Carbon
Castle av., fr. 1734 S. 13th
Cass,W. fr. 12th, bel.Thompson
Cassady's ct., fr. 829 Marriott
Cassion pl., fr. 721 Columbia av
Castle ct., fr. 1036 Sargeant
Castner av., N. fr. Orchard
Castor rd., fr. Oxford rd.,(Fkd.)
Catawba pl., fr. 215 German
Catharine, E. & W. 800 S.
Cathcart ct., fr. 1131 Lombard
Cathedral av., S. fr. Lancaster
  av., ab. 48th
Cattell av., N. fr. Pearl,bel.20th
Cayuga, E. & W. 4400 N.
Caven, S. fr. Hamilton, ab. 19th
Cedar, N. fr. Berks, ab. Gaul
Cedar, N. fr. 4141 Main, (Myk.)
Cedar, N. fr. Meadow, (Fkd.)
Cedar Hill, (Myk.)
Cedar la., E. fr. Haines, (Gtn.)
Celeste, W. fr. 2d bel. Moore
Cemetery, fr. 3423 Indiana av.,
Central pl., W. fr. 5th, ab. Race
Central Buildings, N. fr. Pear

Centre, fr. 4957 Gtn. av., (Gtn.)
Centre, W. fr. 36th, ab. Market
Centre, fr. 4547 Main, (Myk.)
Ceruse, S. fr. Stone, ab. 15th
Chadwick, S. fr. Reed, ab. 16th
Chadwick pl., fr. 858 N. 4th
Chalfonte, fr. 3112 Hamilton
Chambers' av., fr. 2015 Carlton
Champion pl., E. fr. Dunton
Chance pl., fr. 327 New Market
Chancellor,W.fr.32d,ab.Walnut
Chancellor, fr. 214 S. 16th
Chancery la., fr. 126 Arch
Chandler's ct., fr. 1011 Palmer
Chant, fr. 23 S. 10th
Chapman, fr. 751 S. Front
Charles, S. fr. South, ab. 4th
Charles, N. fr. Federal, ab. 6th
Charles pl., fr. 427 Rugan
Charlotte, N. fr. Brown, ab 3d
Charter fr. 2304 Amber
Chartner, fr. 321 N. 24th
Chatham, S. fr. Green, ab. 5th
Chatham, fr 823 E. Lehigh av.
Chauncey, S. fr. Stiles, ab. 18th
Chelton av., fr. Gtn. av.(Gtn,)
Chenango, E. & W., fr. Sophia
Cherry, W. fr. 3d, ab. Arch
Cherry, N. fr. Meadow, (Fkd.)
Chester, fr. 815 Race
Chestnut, E. & W. 100 S.
Chestnut, N. fr. Gtn. av. (Gtn.)
Chesnut, N. fr. Main, (Myk.)
Chestnut av., E. fr. Castle st
Chestnut pl., fr. 3520 Sansom,
Chew, E. & W., 5800 N.
China, fr. 1018 S. Front
China, S. fr. Green, ab. 4th
Chippewa, N. fr. South, ab. 26th
Cholladay's ct., fr. Sheaff's al.
Christian. E. & W., 900 S.
Christy pl., fr. 917 St. John
Chubb, S. fr. Federal, ab. 8th
Church, fr. 319 N. 3d
Church, W. fr. 7th, ab. York
Church, fr. 1322 Fitzwater
Church, fr. 226 S. 37th
Church, N. fr. Chestnut, (Myk.)
Church,fr.Frankford,av.(Fkd.)
Church, av., S. fr. Watts
Church la., fr.5477Gtn.av.(Gtn.)
Church pl., fr. 1122 Lombard
Churnard,N.fr.Tioga,ab.Myrtle
Cinnaminson la., N. fr. Washington, (Myk.)
Citron, W. fr. 11th, ab. Wallace
Clarkson, E. & W., 2600 N.
Clarion, S. fr. Tioga
Claffin's ct., fr. 1319 Heath
Claghorn pl., Front, ab. Poplar
Clairborn, fr. 1215 Ball
Clapier, S. fr. Morris, (Gtn.)
Clare, fr. 528 Carpenter

Clarion, fr. 251 N. 41st,
Clarion, S. fr. Federal, ab. 13th
Clarissa, pl., fr. 538 Linden
Clarm nt, E. fr.45th ab, Eadline
Clark, N. fr. Lefevre, (Bdg.)
Clark, fr. 1024 S. 3d
Clark's av., fr. 418 Buttonwood
Clarkson pl., fr. 530 Linden
Clawge's ct., N. fr. Mulberry al
Clay, W. fr. 11th, ab. Green
Clayton, W. fr. Cherry, ab. 20th
Clayton, fr. 728 N. 22d
Clearfield, E. & W. 3100 N.
Clematis av, fr., 114 Christian
Colebrook pl., 772 S. Front
Coleman, fr. 2120 Dickerson
Clemantine, E. fr. 3119 Emerald
Clement,S.fr.Carpenter,ab.16th
Clemmon's al., Race, ab. 11th
Cliff pl., fr. 1424 Race
Clifford, fr. 1823 N. 3d
Clifford al., Front ab. Market
Clifton, S. fr. Seymour, (Gtn.)
Clifton, S. fr. South, ab. 10th
Clinton, N. fr. McFarran
Clinton, W. fr. 9th, ab. Pine
Clinton av., fr. 1921 Pearl
Clinton av., fr. Bringhurst, (Gtn.)
Clinton ct., fr. 457 Franklin
Clivedon,av.N fr.Gtn.av. (Gtn.)
Close, W fr. 5th ab. McKean
Clover, f. 12 h, ab. Chestnut
Clyde al. S. fr. Race, ab. 5th
Clymer, W. fr. Campbell
Cobb N. fr. Queen, ab. 4th
Coburn, N. fr. South, ab. 2d
Coffin's ct., E. fr. 2d, ab. Race
Cohen pl., fr, 812 S. Front
Cohocksink, fr. 729 Parrish
Colchester, fr. 831 Charlotte
Collum, N. fr. Gtn. av., (Gtn.)
Collard al., fr. Farron pl
Columbia av., E. & W. 1700 N
Columbia ct., fr. Landreth
Columbia row,fr.2019 N. fr. 12th
Comber's ct., S. fr Linton
Commerce, W. fr. 22 N. 4th
Commerce, N,fr. York & Moyer
Commissioner av.. 3129 Gaul
Compromise, E fr.17th ab. Pine
Conard's ct., fr. 1617 Becket
Conarroe. (Mky.)
Concord,W. fr. 2d,ab. Catherine
Concord pl., N. fr. Concord
Concordia av., N. fr. Concord
Conestoga pl., fr. 1445 Cadwalder
Conestoga, S. fr. Paschall, ab. 54th
Congress, E. fr. 2d ab. Catherine
Conlin's ct., fr. 1325 Heath
Connelly ct., fr. 521 Christian

Conrow ct. fr. 105 Chenango
Conway ct., fr. 311 New Market
Coombes, fr. 44 N. Front
Cook, N. fr. Pine, ab. 16th
Cooke, E. fr. Tulip, bel. Berks
Cooper, W. fr. Dixeys
Cooper, N. fr. Ontario, bel. 2d
Cope, N. fr. Locust, ab. 23d
Cope's al , E. fr. 129 S. Water
Copia, fr. 810 S. 16th
Corinthian av.,S. fr. College av. ab. 20th
Corn, N. fr. Reed
Corwin pl., fr 312 Front
Cottage, N. fr. Cedar (Gtn.)
Cottage, W. fr. Front, ab. South
Cottingham pl., fr 5 9 Federal
Cotton, fr. Main, (Myk)
Coulter, N. E. fr. 36th & Queen
Coulston, E. fr. Thouron
Court al., fr. 722 Beach
Courtland av., fr. 330 New Market
Courtland, E. & W. 4600 N
Courtland, S. fr. Tucker, (Fkd.)
Coyle pl., fr. 607 St. Mary
Cowley, fr. 256 N, 13th
Cowper, fr. Hight's ct
Cowperthwait av., fr. 327 New
Cowsl'p, W. fr. 15th, ab. Race
Cox, S. W. fr. 17th, ab. Pine
Cox ct., fr. 220 Acorn al
Cox ct., fr. 15 N. 9th
Cox's ct., fr. 1119 Ohio
Cozzen's av. E. fr. 931 Rachel
Cozen, E. fr. 13th bel. Carpenter
Craig's av.,N. fr. Shackamaxon
Craig's ct., fr. 615 Filbert
Craig's pl , E. fr. Raspberry
Crammer pl., fr. 930 N. 3d
Crane fr. 521 N. 4th
Crane's ct , fr. 130 Mead
Cran's ct., fr. 843 Marriott
Craven, fr. 216 N. Front
Crawford's ct., fr. 506 N. Front
Crawford, fr. 2522 Gaul
Crawford, fr. 3610 Ridge av.
Crease, fr. 1422 Frankford av
Cresheim rd., fr. Carpenter; (Gtn.)
Cresson, W. fr. 5th, ab. Arch
Cresson, W. fr. Green la. (Myk.)
Crockett's ct., fr. 28 S. 5th
Crooked Billet pl., fr.21 S.Water
Crooked pl., fr. 467 New Market
Croskey, fr. 2217 Columbia av.
Cross, W. fr. 8th, ab. Tasker
Cross al., fr. 723 St. Mary
Cross al. S. fr. Green, ab 4th
Crown, N. fr. Race, ab. 4th
Crown pl., fr. 312 N. Front
Crowson, W. fr. Mill, (Gtn.)
Crowther's ct., fr. 607 S. Juniper

Cuba, S. fr. Morris, bel. 4th
Cuba pl., fr. 116 Poplar
Culbertson's ct., fr. 1616 Fairmount av.
Cullen W. fr. 7th, ab. South
Culp av., S. fr. Cuyler
Culvert, N. E. fr. Poplar, ab.4th
Culvert, W. fr. 3240 Cedar
Culvert, fr. Metcalf
Cumbach, W. fr. 12th, bel. Reed
Cumberland, E,W. 2500 N.
Cumberland, E.fr. Armat,(Gtn)
Cunningham av., fr. 1112 Federal
Curfew, fr. 3925 Aspen
Curran pl., E. fr. 4th, ab. Green
Currant al.,N.fr.Spruce,ab.10th
Currant, W. fr. 1914 Cedar
Curry's ct., fr. 1109 Bainbridge
Curtin, E. & W. 3200 S.
Cuscaden's ct., fr. 1109 German
Cuthbert, W. fr. 11th, bel. Arch
Cuyler, fr. 426 N. 19th
Cypress, E. fr. 4th, ab. Pine
D. N. fr. Kensington av., ab.C,
Dacota, W. fr. 9th ab. Dauphin
Dahl's, N. fr. Olive, ab. 13th
Daisy av.,W. fr. 18th, ab. South
Dale, S. fr. Lehigh av., bel. 15th
Dallas al., fr. 38 S. 13th
Dallett's ct., fr. 1320 Silver
Dallett's ct., fr. 410 Rugan
Daly's ct., fr. 1339 Olive,
Damon, N. fr. Indiana, ab. 34th
Dana, E. fr. 2d, ab. Noble
Daniel pl., fr. 1339 Earl
Dannaker's av., fr. 227 N. 3d
Danver pl , fr. 137 New
Darcy, fr. 714 Spafford
Darien, N. fr. Brown. ab. 8th
Darling pl., fr. 324 Willow
Darragh's, fr. 233 Lybrand
Dart, pl., fr. 1119 Hamilton
Dart, W. fr. 1412 Hity
Darwin,W. fr. 15th, ab. Howard
Dauphin, E. & W. 2900 N.
Davenport, fr. 2506 S. 9th
Davidson, fr. 1140 St. John
Davidson pl., fr. 985 Marshall
Davis, S. E. fr. Gtn. av., (Gtn.)
Davis, fr. 1210 N. 12th
Davis av., fr. 145 N. 8th
Davis ct., fr. 1532 Lombard
Davis ct., N. fr. Race, ab. 23d
Davis ct., fr. 604 Fairmount av.
Davis pl., S. fr. Alaska, ab. 13th
Dawson pl., fr. 1304 Pearl
Day, fr. 27 Thompson,
Dayton, W. fr. 6th, ab. Green
Deacon, fr. 1111 Girard av.
Deagen pl., fr. 619 Tamarind
Deal, fr, 1737 Frankford av.
Deal av., S. fr. Deal

Dean, fr. 1212 Walnut
Dean, fr. 1218 Mifflin
Dean's av., N. fr. Day
Decatur, fr. 616 Market
Dedaker's ct., fr. 27 Otter
Deimling pl., fr. 236 Un on
DeKalb, ct., fr. Aspen, ab. 37th
DeKalb's ct., fr. 960 Warnock
Delancey pl., 326 S. 18th
Dayman, fr. 3319 Clearfield
Delaney pl., fr. 743 S. 7th
Delaware av., N. and S. along Delaware river
Delaware, fr. 3230 N. 20th
Delhi, N. fr. Diamond, ab. 9th
Delta pl., fr. 1343 Olive
Demar pl., fr. 110 Bainbridge
Demster pl., fr. 1518 Barclay
Denmark, E. fr. 2d, bel. Tasker
Denny's ct., fr. 425 Marriott
Depot, fr. 540 N. 8th
Depot, S. E. fr. Gtn. ave. (Gtn.)
Deringer av , fr. 1513 N. Front
Deschong, fr. 1220 S. 25th
Desilver's ct., fr. 428 Walnut
Desota, fr. 1238 Struthers
Devitt's av , fr. 1128 St. John
Devon pl., fr. 319 Fairmount av.
Dexter, E. fr. Green la., (Myk.)
Dial, W. fr. 5th, ab. Morris
Diami, E. fr. Liscomb. ab. 23d
Diamond, E. & W., 2100 N.
Diamond, S. fr. Brinton
Diamond ct., fr. 618 South
Dickenson, fr. 2519 Commerce
Dickerson, E. & W., 1500 S.
Dickson's al., fr. 716 S. 7th
Dickson's pl., fr. 907 N. Broad
Diligent av., fr. 916 Buttonwood
Dilk's ct., fr. 904 Wood
Dillwyn, N. fr. Vine, ab. 3d
Dilmore, S. fr. McKean, ab.9th
Dingler's ct., fr. 116 Van Horn
Discount pl., fr. 32 N. 6th
District pl , E. fr. 10th, ab. Vine
Divan pl , fr. 117 Fairmount av.
Division, fr. 410 N. 11th
Divine's ct . fr. 2015 Naudain
Division, fr. 2123 Cedar
Division, fr. Sharpneck, (Gtn.)
Division, E. fr. Main, (Myk )
Dixey, fr. 2011 Locust
Dixey's ct., fr. 1632 Lombard
Doaks, fr. 1122 Bainbridge
Dobbins, W. fr. 18th, ab. Pine
Dock, S. E. fr. 3d, ab. Walnut
Dodge pl., N. fr. Metcalf, ab. 2d
Doll's ct., fr. 1036 St. John
Doman's pl., fr. 235 Christian
Donley, fr. 922 S. 10th
Donnegan's ct., fr. 715 St. John
Donneganna, fr. 1218 S. 15th
Donnelly, fr. 833 Marriott

Donnelly's ct., fr. 1817 South
Dorrence, fr. 1820 Carpenter
Dorsey, fr. 728 Spafford
Dorsey, fr. 412 S. 13th
Dott, N. fr. Jefferson, ab. 20th
Dougherty's al., fr. 514 South
Dougherty's ct., fr. 730 Alaska
Douglass, fr. 3118 Haverford
Douglas av., fr. 1230 Brown
Dove ct., fr. 806 Duane
Dove pl., fr. 1012 S. 3d
Dover, S. fr. York, ab. 28th
Dover ct., fr. 914 Poplar
Downing, fr. 2021 Callowhill
Doyle, fr. 521 S. 15th
Doyle's ct., E. fr. 3d, bel. South
Drayson pl., fr. 1123 P.ne
Drayton, fr. 1232 Rye
Dreer, W. fr. Amber, ab. Norris
Dreer's ct., fr. 323 Griscom
Drinker, E. fr. 2d, ab. Arch
Drum's av., fr. 808 Buttonwood
Drury, W. fr. 13th, ab. Sansom
Drydan pl., fr. 228 E. Thompson
Duane, fr. 1225 Brown
Duberry ct., fr. 519 Brooks
Dubree, fr. 1821 Wylie
Duck al., S. E. fr. Mattis
Dudley, W. fr. 5th, ab. McKean
Dudley pl., fr. 512 Christian
Duffey's ct., fr. 723 Hubbell
Duffy ct , fr. Crane, ab. 13th
Dugan, fr. 1512 Spruce
Dugan's ct., fr. 330 Master
Duncan, fr. Tacouy, (Fkd.)
Dungan's av., W. fr. 2d, ab. Otter
Dunlap, S. fr. Chestnut, ab. 22d
Dunn's ct., fr. 759 S. 6th.
Dunsdal pl., fr. 2048 Lombard
Dunton, from 19 Otter
Duponceau, fr. 818 Walnut
Durham pl., fr. 517 Race
Duross ct., fr. 784 6th
Duross pl., fr. 819 N. 13th
Durrs' ct., W. fr. Orchard
Dutton, N. fr. Mifflin, bel. Front
Dutton's ct., fr. 620 Washington av
Dutilh, fr. 412 Conn
Duval, N. fr. Adams, (Gtn.)
Dyott's ct., fr. 1921 Franklin
Dyre, Frankford av., (Fkd.)
**E.** N. fr. Kensington av., ab. D
Eadline, fr. 420 N. 32d
Eagen pl., fr. 1005 Hamilton
Eagle, fr. 1051 Leopard
Eagle, W. fr. 4029 Lancaster av
Eagle av., fr. 1220 N. Front
Eagleston, E. fr. Burnett
Earl, W. fr. 24th, bel. Brown
Earl, fr. 742 Thompson,
Earp, W. fr. 8th, ab. Reed

Earp, fr. 520 N. 19th
East, N. E. fr. Cresson, (Myk.)
East ct., fr. 331 Griscom
East ct, fr. 1416 Spring Garden
East, fr. 940 N. Delaware av
Eastwick av., fr. 1612 Ogden
Eaton pl , N. fr. Eagle
Eden pl., 224 Catharine
Edgar pl., S. fr. Pine, ab. 9th
Edgemont, N. fr. Allegheny av., ab. Salmon
Edgeley. N. E. fr. 33d, & Oxford
Edina pl., fr. 1034 N. 4th
Edisto pl., fr. 614 Vincent
Edward, E. fr. 2d, ab. Otter
Edward, S. fr. Pine, (Fkd.)
Edward, fr. Haverford, ab. 31st
Edwin, fr. 1720 Ridge av
Edmund, S. fr. Bridge, (Fkd.)
Effingham, N. fr. 615 Tasker,
Eisen av., W. fr. 4th, ab. Master
Elba pl., fr. 909 Ontario
Elba pl., fr. 965 Beach
Elbow la., W. fr. Bank
Elder, S. fr. Morgan, ab. 10th
Eldridge pl., fr. 1817 N. 6th
Elfreth's al., E. fr. 2d, ab. Arch
Elgin pl., fr. 1210 Heath
Eliza, W. fr. 15th, bel. Master
Eliza av., fr. 818 N. 12th
Elizabeth, N. fr. Church, (Fkd.)
Elizabeth pl., fr. 1423 Hope
Elizabeth, fr. 2630 Emerald
Elk, fr. Otter, ab. Front
Elkhart, fr. Melvale, ab. Maple
Ella, fr. 2304 Amber
Ella, N. fr. Cambria, bel. Fillmore
Ellen, fr. 928 N. Front
Ellen pl., E. fr. Front ab. Mead
Ellet's av., N. fr. Race, ab. 5th
Elliott's ct , fr. 732 Lombard
Ellis, S, fr. Wallace, ab. 9th
E'lis' ct., fr. 1030 Sansom
Ellison, S fr. Peter's al
Ellison, W. fr. Mechanic,(Myk.)
Ellison pl., N. fr. Vine, ab. 11th
Ellis, fr. Mechanic, (Myk.)
Ellsworth, W. fr. 1118 S. 8th
Elm, fr. 1420 Wildey
Elmwood av., S. W. fr. Gibsons
Elm av., W. fr. 4000 Girard av
Elmslie's al., fr. 220 S. 2d
Eltonhead ct., fr. 2114 Wood
Emery, fr. 115 Bokius, (Bdg.)
Ellwood la., fr. 2730 N. 2d
Elwyn, S. fr. Race, ab. 9th
Ely, N. fr. Locust, ab. 10th
Ely av. fr. 410 Carpenter
Ely av., W. fr. 12th ab. Brown
Emanuel pl., fr. 317 Monroe
Ember av N. fr. Heath, ab. 13th
Emden, fr. 625 Bainbridge

Emerald, fr. 2101 N. Front
Emeline, fr. 616 S. 8th
Emlen, W. fr. Upsal, (Gtn.)
Emeline, fr. 419 E. Lehigh av.
Emlin, E. fr. Gaul, bel. Adams
Emma, N. fr. Burgess
Emmet, W. fr. 3d, bel. Wharton
Emory, fr. 1533 E. Thompson
Engle, E. fr. Gtn. av. (Gtn.)
Englefreid, W. fr. Elm av.
English, N. fr. Powell, ab. 5th
Ennis pl., fr. 2307 Vine
Ennos, fr. Fraley ct.
Enue, W. fr. 7th ab. Wharton
Enquirer, fr. 1119 Brown
Enterprize, W. fr. 4th, ab. Tasker
Enuc, fr. 1221 S. 7th
Eppright's ct., fr. 1408 S. Front
Erdman, fr. 1721 Perkioman
Erdman's ct., fr. 820 N. Front
Erety, W. fr. 16th ab. Spruce
Ericsson, fr. 920 South 9th
Erie av., E. & W., 3700 N
Erie, fr. 1018 Bainbridge
Ernst, fr. 1528 S. 9th
Esher, N. fr. Girard av. ab. 27th
Esher av., fr. 1209 Fairmount av
Eshner pl., N. fr. 1007 Charlotte
Espy. fr. 1326 Fitzwater
Essex, N. fr. Christian, ab. 8th
Essex al., fr. 245 Quince
Eutaw, S. fr. Race, ab. 7th
Estaugh, fr. 3420 N. 20th
Eustis, W. fr. 4th, ab. Mifflin
Evangelist, fr. 720 S. 7th
Evans, S. fr. Centre, (Gtn.)
Evans, fr. 441 E. Clearfield
Evans av., S. fr. Vine, ab. 22d
Evans, N. fr. Federal, ab. 2d
Evans ct., fr. 706 St. Mary
Eveland, fr. 1029 St. John
Everett, fr. 908 S. 12th
Everett pl. N. fr. Pegg
Evergreen, fr. 740 S. 20th
Ewing's pl., fr. 714 Guilford
Ewald pl., fr. 1811 Naudain
Exchange pl., fr. 240 Chestnut
Exeter, fr. 124 S. 16th
Eyne, fr. Wildey, ab. Palmer
Ezra pl., fr. 312 Catherine
F., W. fr. 22d, ab. Spruce
F., N. fr. Kensington av., ab, E
Faas pl., fr. 1021 Morgan
Fable av., E. fr. 6th, ab. Vine
Factory, W. fr. 23d, ab. Pine
Factory, N. fr. Pine, (Fkd.)
Fail pl., W. fr. Rachel, ab. Brown
Fairbank pl., fr. Levant
Fairchild pl., fr. 1122 Palmer
Fairfax pl., fr. 129 S. 5th
Fairfield, fr. 18 N. 20th
Fairlamb pl., fr. 928 Torr

Fairhill, fr. 524 Allegheny av.
Fairmount av., E. & W. 700 N
Fairman pl., fr. 917 Torr
Farina, fr. Penn, (Fkd.)
Fall pl., N. fr. Race ab. 5th
Fallon, S. fr. Fitzwater ab. 8th
Fame ct., fr. 21 Laurel
Fareira's ct., fr. 1013 Barclay
Farie's ct., fr. 122 N. Front
Farner's pl., fr. 1628 Philip
Farrell pl., fr. 1317 Lawrence
Farrell, fr. 1021 McKean
Farson pl., fr. 1028 Beach
Faulkner, S. fr. Marriott. ab. 3d
Fawn, N. fr. Moss, ab. 6th
Fawn, N. fr. Master, ab. 12th
Fawn av., fr. 1624 Fawn
Fayette, fr. 918 Arch
Fearon av., fr. 1818 Naudian
Federal, E. & W., 1200 S.
Feinour pl., fr. 736 Swanson
Fell, fr. 1828 N. 19th
Felton, W. fr. 30th, ab. Park av.
Felton, fr. 129 Mead
Ferguson's ct., fr. 1334 South
Fernon, W. fr. 8th, ab. Morris
Ferris ct., fr. 220 N. Front
Fetter's la., fr. 117 N, 3d
Field, W. fr. 10th, bel. McKean
Fields, N. fr. Francis, ab. 16th
Fife's pl., fr. 1417 Bainbridge
Fifty Acre la., (Fkd.)
Filbert, W. fr. 6th, ab. Market
Filch, fr. 2120 Race
Fillmore, fr. 1730 Cox
Fillmore av., fr. 128 N. 15th
Fillmore, fr. Willow, (Fkd.)
Filson, N. fr. Arch, ab. 22d
Finch, S. fr. Dauphin, ab. 13th
Finnegan's ct., fr. 717 Baker
Finney's ct., fr. 631 Lombard
Firth, fr. 2521 Kensington av
Firth ct., fr. 919 Hamilton
Fisher, fr. 1612 S. 6th
Fishbourne, pl., fr. 634 Washington av.
Fisher, fr. 1929 E. Clearfield
Fisher's ct., fr. 1319 Atmore
Fisher's la., fr. Gtn. av. (Gtn.)
Fisher's pl., fr. 1321 Charlotte
Fitter, fr. 1731 N. 2d
Fitzpatrick pl., fr. 615 St. Mary
Fitzwater, W. fr. 729 Passyunk
Flanigan's ct., fr. 1336 Beach
Fleet, fr. 521 Locust
Fletcher, fr. 2220 N. 25th
First, fr. 20 N. 23d
Fleason, N. fr. Wood, (Myk.)
Fleming, W. fr. 21st, ab. Market
Flickwir's pl., fr. 227 German
Fling's pl., fr. 1250 Hope
Flood's pl., fr. 912 S. 6th
Florence, fr. 1715 North

Florence, S. fr. Milton, ab. 10th
Florida, N. fr. Haverford av.
Florida, fr. 1113 Catherine
Florist, fr. 220 N. Front
Flower, fr. 720 New Market
Flora, W. fr. Reed, ab. 9th
Ford, N. fr. Pine, ab. 19th
Forder av., fr. 1213 Silver
Forrest pl., fr. 123 S. 4th
Forrest pl., fr. 621 Guilford
Foster, W. fr. 32d, bel. Arch
Foster's row, fr. 1221 Sorral
Fothergill, S. fr. Pine, ab. 9th
Foulkrod, E. fr Leiper, (Fkd.)
Fountain, fr. 2018 N. 15th
Fountain, fr. 1618 S. 8th
Fox, W. fr. Gaul, ab. Serrill
Fox, fr. 29 E. Cumberland
Fox's ct., fr. 1215 South
Fox's ct., fr. 1218 Fitzwater
Frampton pl.,fr.1013 Nectarine
Francis, S. fr. Ridge av ,ab.16th
Francis pl., fr. 843 Marriott
Francis, fr. 1120 S. 12th
Franconi pl., fr. 721 N. 9th
Frank, S. fr. Quincy, (Gtn.)
Frank's ct., fr. 467 Franklin
Frankford,N.fr. Adams, (Fkd.)
Frankford av., N. W. fr. Laurel
Franklin, N. fr. Race, ab. 7th
Franklin, fr. 5426 Gtn.av.(Gtn.)
Franklin, fr. 23d, ab. Pine
Franklin, N. fr. Pine, (Fkd.)
Franklin ct., fr. 522 Franklin
Flickwersel, fr. 219 German
Frederick, W. fr.20th,ab.Mifflin
French, W.fr. 16th, ab Park av
French, fr. 4034 Baring
Free, fr. 2219 S. 7th
Freed's av., S. fr. Race. ab. 7th
Freeman's ct., W. fr. Quince
Freeston pl., fr. 1007 Moyamensing av.
Fremont, fr. 2820 Salmon
Freytag pl., fr. 519 Alaska
Freidlander, fr. 2026 Race
Friendship ct., fr. 621 St. John
Fries ct., fr. 18 N. 11th
Fromer's ct., fr. 924 Rodman
Front, N. & S. bel. 2d
Front, fr. 4050 Frankford,(Fkd.)
Fulton, fr. 746 S. 12th
Fulton, S. fr. Race, ab. 22d
Fulton, W. fr. 2821 Tulip
Fulton, fr. 1117 Hewson
Furlong ct., fr. 707 Cherry
Furness, N. fr. Branch
G., W. fr. 22d, ab. Spruce
G., N. fr. Kensington av., ab. F
Gadsby pl., fr. 1722 Lombard
Gafiney's av., fr. 632 Fitzwater
Gaine's pl., fr. 239 Queen
Galena, S. fr. Gaskill, ab. 4th

Gale's ct., fr. 759 Passyunk av.
Galbraith's ct., fr. 530 New Market
Gallager's ct., fr. 1622 Alaska
Gallatin pl., fr. 119 China
Galloway, fr. 309 George
Galloway, fr. 1218 S. 25th
Garber pl,, fr. 403 New Market
Garden, N. fr. Jenks, (Bdg.)
Garden, N. fr. Vine, ab. 8th
Gampher av., fr. 505 Catherine
Garibaldi, fr. 3418 N. 10th
Garside, N. fr. Race, ab. 2d
Garvin pl., fr. 236 Catherine
Garden, N. fr. Berks, ab. Tulip
Garden, N. fr. Myrtle, ab. 49th
Garnet, fr. 1915 Jefferson
Garnet, S. fr. Hart's la.
Garreston pl., fr. 827 S. 3d
Garside, fr. 1422 N. 23d
Gascon av., fr. 320 New Market
Gaskill, W. fr. 2d, ab. South
Gatzmer, fr. 121 S. 2d
Gaul, fr. 221 E. Montgomery av.
Gayton pl., fr. 1207 Kater
Gay, fr. 4771 Cresson (Myk.)
Gay's ct., fr. 1242 N. 3d
Geary, E. & W., 3300 S
Geary, fr. Faires ct.
Geary av., fr. 208 Richmond
Gebhard, fr. 1521 Race
Gebhart ct., fr. 1628 Carlton
Gegan, N. fr. Norris, ab. 4th
Geisler, fr. 3022 Salmon
Geiss, fr. 558 E. Dauphin
Genoese pl., fr. 319 Master
George, W. fr. 2d, 1100 N.
George ct., fr. 605 Sansom
German, W. 732 S. 2d
Germantown av.fr.1020N.Front
Gerrett, W. fr. 18th, bel. Reed
Gerker, fr. Columbia av., ab. Thompson
Gerrill, fr. 2519 N. Broad
Getz, N. fr. McKean, ab. 10th
Getzell pl., fr. 1221 Poplar
Gibson's av., fr. Baltimore av
Gibson's ct., fr. 819 Charlotte
Gideon's ct., N. fr. Wood, ab.8th
Gifford pl., N. fr. Ogden,ab.16th
Gihon pl., fr. 1232 Carlisle
Gilbert, W. fr. Kessler to 10th
Garrison ct., E. fr. Andrew
Gilboy ct., E. fr. 2d, ab. Poplar
Gillespie ct., fr. 1340 South
Giles, W. fr. 23d ab. Oxford
Gillingham, W. fr. Cadwalader
Gillingham,fr.Mulberry,(Fkd.)
Gillis al., N. fr. South, ab 5th
Gill's av., S. fr. Poplar, ab. 12th
Gill's pl., fr. 728 Bainbridge
Gilmore pl. fr. 926 St. John
Gilpin, E. fr. 17th, ab. Chestnut

Gilpin pl., fr. 840 Lawrence
Ginnodo, E. fr. 19th ab. Poplar
Girard, W. fr. 20 S. 11th
Girard av., E. & W.,1200 N
Given pl., fr. 221 Christian
Given's ct., fr. 2017 Filbert
Gladding pl., fr. 724 N. 13th
Glaney pl., N. fr. Noble, ab.10th
Glasgow pl.,S. fr. Poplar, ab. 2d
Glasmire pl., fr. 321 Orchard
Glass ct., fr. 1422 Brainbridge
Glazier pl., E. fr.3d, ab. Poplar
Glenat's ct., fr. 33 Poplar
Glenville pl., fr. 828 N. 15th
Glenwood, N. fr. Pegg
Glenwood av.,N.E.fr.317 Master
Gloucester pl., fr. 1070 Frankford av.
Godey, N. fr. Wall, ab. 5th
Godfrey, fr. Lehman, (Gtn.)
Godfrey, fr, 1610 S. 2d
Godfrey av., fr. 409 Jefferson
Gold, W. fr. 2d, ab. Walnut
Gold, fr. 2327 Pennsylvania av.
Gold, E. fr. Cedar, ab. Ann
Goldbeck, fr. 1131 N. 2d
Goldbeck, fr. 1224 N. 21st.
Goldsmith, ct., fr. 911 Rachel
Goldsmith ct.,518 New Market
Golser, ct., fr. 1225 N. Front
Gonsha, N. fr. Lisbon, ab. 5th
Good, W. fr. Gtn. av., (Gtn.)
Goodbread pl., fr. 1004 Vernon
Goodman, S. fr. Rising Sun la.
Goodman's ct., fr. 319 N. Market
Goodwater, E.fr. 8th, ab. Locust
Goodwill al., fr. 1328 Race
Goodwill ct., 1310 Race
Goodwin pl., fr. 1834 Beach
Gordon, fr. Geiss
Gordon's ct., fr. 1012 Rodman
Gordon's pl., fr. 1831 Naudain
Gore's ct., fr. 322 Bainbridge
Gorgas, E. fr. Gtn. av., (Gtn.)
Gorrel's ct., fr. 920 S. 5th
Goshen av.,W. fr. 11th, ab. Pine
Goss ct., S. fr. Emeline
Gossamer av., fr. 1017 Noble
Gothic, E. fr. 2d., ab. Walnut
Goujon's pl., fr. 920 Marshall
Govett's ct., fr. 915 Rodman
Gowen's la., fr Gtn. av.(Gtn.)
Grace, W. fr. 16th, ab. Arch
Graff, W. fr. 11th, ab. Race
Grafton, E. fr. 829 Fallon,
Grafton ct., fr. 817 S. 5th
Graham, fr. 1315 N. 19th
Grament pl., fr. 829 Carpenter
Grampian pl. fr. 713 N. 13th
Grant, W. fr. 9th, ab. Mifflin
Granite, fr. 216 S. Front
Granville, W. fr. 21st, ab. Pine
Grape, fr. 414 N. 33d

Grape, fr. 4841 Main, (Myk.)
Gratz, N. fr. Oxford, ab. 18th
Gravel ct., fr. 1318 Olive
Graver's la., fr. Gtn. av. (Gtn.)
Gray, fr. 121 Poplar
Graydon, N. fr. Cowslip
Gray's Ferry rd., fr. 2230 Sou. h
Grayson, fr. 720 N. 17th
Greaves ct., fr. 1311 Cadwalader
Grcen, E. & W. 600 N.
Green, N. fr. Manheim, (Gtn.),
Green, fr. 3229 Gtn. av.
Green's ct., fr. 624 St. John
Green's ct., fr. 512 St. Mary
Greenhill, fr. 1620 Master
Green la., fr. 4501 Main, (Myk.)
Greenock pl., fr. 1115 Mark's la.
Green's ct., W. fr. 8th, ab. Race
Greenville pl., fr. Vaughan
Greenwich, fr. 1528 S. Front
Greenwood pl., fr. 629 N. Front
Greer, W. fr. Adrian, nr Otis
Grim's av., W. fr. 3d, ab. Poplar
Grim's ct., E. fr. 3d, ab. Poplar
Grim's ct., fr. 1115 Lawrence
Grindstone al., fr. 220 Market
Grinnel pl., fr. 1420 Bainbridge
Griscom, N. fr. Pine, ab. 4th
Griswald al. fr. 5 2 Metcalf
Grove, fr. 1812 Perkiomen
Grover, fr. 110 Queen
Gross, W. fr. 27th, ab. Poplar
Grubb, E. fr. Sycamore
Grum's ct., fr. 1731 Jones
Guate, N. fr. Tioga, ab. 9th
Gucke's ct., fr. 830 St. John
Guest, W. fr. 32d, ab. Oxford
Guilford, fr. 226 South
Gulielma, E. fr. 15th, ab. South
Gummery, S. fr. 212 Alta
Gurney, N. W. fr. Leamy
Guy's Block, E. fr. 309 S. 22d
Guy's ct., S. fr. Spruce, ab. 21st
Gwinn, E. fr. Main, (Myk.)
Gwynn. S. fr. Spruce, ab. 21st
Gwynn's pl.,E.fr.1023 Charlotte
H., N. fr. Kensington av. ab. G
Haas, N. fr. Somerset, ab. 22d
Haas' pl., E. fr. 711 N. 3d
Hacker's pl., fr. 912 S. 4th
Hacket's ct., fr. 438 Monroe
Hackley, W. fr. 4th, ab. Berks
Haddon pl ,S. fr. Poplar ab. 7th
Hagedorn pl., N fr. Lynd, ab.4th
Hagert, W. fr. 22d, ab. York
Hagner, N fr. South, ab. 11th
Hahn, N, fr. Reed, ab. 20th
Hahn's ct., fr. 1921 Cuthbert
Haines, N. fr. 12th, ab. Poplar
Haines, N. fr.5033 Gtn.av,(Gtn.)
Haines' ct.,S.fr.Lemon, ab. 10th
Haines' pl., N. fr. Kates
Hale's ct., N. fr. Federal, ab, 9th

Hale, N. fr. Columbia av. ab 3d
Hall, fr. 920 S. 9th
Hamilton, fr. 1328 N. Front
Hansberry, fr. Gtn. av. (Gtn.)
Hanley's ct., fr. Gtn. av. (Gtn.)
Halleck pl., fr. 1320 Charlotte
Hallowell, fr. 1030 S. 6th
Hammell's ct., fr. 1710 Lombard
Hamilton, W. fr. 9th ab. Noble
Hamilton, W. fr. Green la. (Myk)
Hamlet's pl., fr. 1220 Hope
Hammit's av., N. fr. Crease
Hampton, W. fr. 20th, bel. Pine
Hance's pl., fr. 1528 Cadwalader
Hancock, N. fr. 129 Girard av.
Hancock, fr. Church la., (Gtn.)
Hand, W. fr. 20th, bel. Pine
Hansell's ct., fr. 1013 Barley
Harberger's pl., fr. 1710 Jones
Harbeson pl., fr. 1313 Callowhill
Hare, W. fr. 720 N. 22d
Harbor, fr. 1022 Frankford av.
Harden ct., S. fr. Pearl, ab. 15th
Harding pl., fr. 322 German
Harlen, W. fr. 19th, ab. Master
Harold, fr. 2620 N. 22d
Harper, W. fr. 28th, ab. Poplar
Harper's ct., fr. 518 S. 18th
Harshaw, fr. 2017 Catherine
Hart, fr. 1822 N. 10th
Hartranft, E. & W., 3400 S.
Hartung, fr. 40 N. 21st
Harvey ct., fr. 408 S. 21st
Harker's pl., fr. 1814 Baker
Harkenson's pl., fr. 713 Baker
Harley's ct., fr. 2011 Market
Harman's al., fr. 2122 Sansom
Harmony, fr. 720 S. 4th
Harmony, W. fr. 3d, ab. Walnut
Harmony ct., fr. 412 S. 6th
Harmstead, fr. 618 S. 19th
Harmstead pl., fr. 912 Ogden
Harper's ct., fr. 2016 Lombard
Harper's pl., 629 Guilford
Harriet, S. fr. Ross, ab. 10th
Harriet pl., fr. 2015 Pearl
Harrison, fr. 1420 Frankford av.
Harrison, N. fr. Gay, (Myk.)
Harrison, E. fr. Penn, (Fkd.)
Harrison ct., fr. Pleasant, (Gtn.)
Harris's ct., f. 18 Letitia
Hartley pl., S. fr. Cherry, ab. 13th
Hartman's ct., fr. Gray's Ferry rd
Hart's la., fr. 2820 Kensington av
Hart's rd., fr. 2616 N. 20th
Harton pl. S fr. Race, ab. 8th
Hartwell av., S. fr. Gtn. av. (C.H.)
Harvey, fr. Gtn av., (Gtn.)
Harvey's ct. W. fr. 2d, bel. Pine
Harvey's pl., fr. 1021 St. John
Haskin pl., fr. 220 Federal
Hassinger av., fr. 118 N. Juniper
Haverford av., W. fr. 500 N. 32d

Haviland pl., fr. 232 N. 8th
Hawthorn av., fr 1719 Barker
Hay, W. fr. 6th ab. Reed
Haydock, fr. 1002 N. Front
Hay's ct., fr. 229 St. John
Hayward pl., fr. 921 Hamilton
Haywood pl., 914 Hamilton
Hazel, fr. 1422 N. Front
Hazel, fr. 912 N, 11th
Hazlewood, fr. 2318 Montrose
Hazzard, fr. 2524 Cedar
Hazzard ct., fr. 1917 Cuthbert
Heath, fr. 920 N. 12th
Heberton ct., fr. 1618 Lombard
Hebrew pl., fr. 321 N. 3d
Heck pl., fr. 931 N. 2d
Heckman pl., fr 817 Willow
Heckroth pl., fr. 610 Weaver
Hedge, N. fr. Unity, (Fkd.)
Hedge pl., fr. 928 Hamilton
Heilig pl., S. fr. Native
Heins, fr. 318 S. 12th
Heiss pl., fr. 423 Moyer
Helena pl,, fr. 215 Christian
Helmuth, fr. 532 S. 16th
Hemlock pl., fr. 1420 South
Hemphill, fr. 811 Carpenter
Hemple ct., fr. 1011 Hamilton
Henck's ct., fr. 816 Rachel
Henderson ct., 1028 South
Henly's ct., fr. 729 Carpenter
Henrietta, fr. 1336 N. 21st
Henrietta av., fr. 1020 Highland
Henry, fr. 1113 Lombard
Henry ct., fr. 1312 Gtn. av.
Hepburn, fr. 1618 Bainbridge
Hepburn pl., fr. 746 Passyunk
Herald pl., fr. Ledger pl.
Herb, fr. 516 N. 19th
Herbert pl., fr. 1221 Silver
Herdman ct., fr. 814 N. 5th
Herman, N. fr. Gtn. av., (Gtn.)
Herman, fr. 2314 N. 19th
Herman ct., W. fr. Griscom
Hermitage, fr. 329 Green, ab. 3d
Hermitage, N. fr. 329 Jackson
Hero pl., fr, 419 Carpenter
Herschel av., N. fr Hand
Hedding, N. fr. North, ab. 15th
Hedleg, fr. 3723 Richmond
Hemberger, fr. 2315 Berks
Henry, fr. 2016 Howell
Henry, fr. 3422 Mascher
Helen, S. fr. Harts la.
Herdman, fr. 1815 Perkiomen
Herds, fr. 1312 Picavi
Herman, N. fr. Reed, ab. 17th
Hewitt pl., W. fr. Quince
Hewson, fr. 2734 Salmon
Heyer pl., W. fr, Levant
Hibberd, fr. 1123 Girard av
Hickey, fr. 1518 Market
Hickory ct., fr. 620 Willow

Hide's ct., fr. 821 Filbert
Higgin's ct., fr. 139 Ca`penter
Higgin's pl., fr. 120 Carpenter
High, N. fr, Gtn. av., (Gtn.)
Highland, fr. 28 N. 10th
Highland av.,S.fr.Gtn.av.(Gtn.)
Highland pl., fr. 1019 Highland
Hight's av., fr. 2509 Callowhill
Hight's ct , fr. 913 Hamilton
Hiland pl., fr. 1420 Cadwalader
Hildeburn, fr. 928 Passyunk av
Hill, fr. 739 S. 15th
Hillerman pl., fr. 321 Garden
Hillsdale, S. fr. Race, ab. 3d
Himmelwright pl., fr. 912 S. 6th
Hine's ct., fr. 220 Christian
Hine's ct., fr. 926 Rodman
Hipple's la.,fr.Ridge av.,(Myk.)
Hobensack pl., 118 Fairm'nt av
Hock pl , fr. 1418 Brown
Hockster, fr. 1020 Hoyt
Hoffman, fr. 920 N. 61st
Hoffman, W. fr. 4th, ab. Morris
Holland, fr. 831 N. 5th
Holland pl., fr. 1019 Parrish
Hollinger, fr. 3122 Columbia av
Hollingsworth, fr. 1720 N. 31st
Holly, fr. 1520 Fitzwater
Holly, N. fr. Aspen, ab. 41st
Holman ct., fr. 319 Otis, ..
Holme's al., E, fr. 2d, ab. Vine
Holt's av., fr. 622 New Market
Home pl., fr, 224 German
Homer av., fr. 223 N. 13th
Hope, fr 117 Canal
Hoopes, fr. Clearfield, ab. Bath
Hopkins, S. fr. Race, ab. 57th
Hopkinson pl.,fr.126 N.Juniper
Horn's ct., fr. 927 St. John
Horstman, fr. 2121 Somerset
Horstman, N. fr. Reed, ab. 4th
Horstman's row, fr. 741 S. 3d
Horstman's ct., fr. 324 German
Horstman's ct., fr.214 Carpenter
Horst's ct., fr. 1428 Cadwalader
Horter, N. fr. Gtn. av., (Gtn.)
Houben's pl., fr. 1127 N. 3d
Housekeeper's ct. fr. 1438 Beach
Houston ct., fr. 938 Rodman
Houten row, fr. 1829 N. 6th
Howard, N. fr. 129 Girard av
Howard, S. fr. Brown, ab. 12d
Howard, fr. 4019, Gtn., av
Howard ct., fr.1623 Hamilton
Howell, W. fr. 32d, ab. Arch
Howell, W. fr. 19th, ab. Pine
Hoyt, E. & W. 3500 S
Hubbell, fr. 1029 Catharine
Hubbs, fr. 1530 N. 20th
Hubert pl., fr 841 N. 5th
Huckel's ct., fr. 131 South
Hudson, fr. 2718 Walker
Hudson, S. fr. Market, ab. 3d

Hughes' pl.,fr. 1118 Jefferson av
Huhn, N. fr. Reed, ab. 20th
Hull, E. fr. Amber, ab. Ann
Hull pl, fr. 812 N. Delaware a.
Hulseman ct., fr. 1240 Fltzwater
Hulseman pl., fr. 1228 N. Front
Humboldt, fr. 2518 N. 22d
Humboldt, fr. 3419 N. 11th
Humes, fr. 508 Bainbridge
Hume's av., fr. 2720 South
Hummell, fr. 1120 S. 22d
Hummell's ct., fr. 941 N. 3d
Humphrey's ct., fr. 1519 Filbert
Hunt's la., fr. 2730 Tulip
Hutchinson ct., fr. 203 Dean
Hunter's ct., fr. 1519 Vine
Hunter's row, fr. 330 S 11th
Huntingdon. E. & W. 2600 N
Hunt's ct.. fr. 825 Charlotte
Hutchison, fr. 921 Poplar
Hutton, fr. 800 N. 35th
Huron pl., fr. 1428 Phillip
Hurley, S. fr. Indiana, ab. D
Hurst, fr. 513 South
Hydra pl., fr. 419 Noble
I, N. fr. Kensington av., ab. H
Ida, 1928, S. 31st
Illinois, S. fr. Locust, ab. 17th
Increase ct., fr. 1022 Sansom
Indiana, E. & W. 3000 N
Institute. fr. 1726 Columbia av
Innes, W. fr. 112 Allen
Ingersoll, fr. 1424 N. 18th
Ingle, E. fr. Haines, (Gtn.)
Ingliss, E. fr. 2d. ab. Walnut
Ingram, fr. 1218 S. 27th
Inquirer, fr. 1123 Brown
Iowa av. S. fr. Union, ab. 2d
Iranstan, fr. 411 German
Ireland, S. fr. Harrison
Ireland's ct., fr. 718 Brook
Iron pl., fr. 88 Laurel
Irvin, S. fr. Howell, (Bdg.)
Irvin, fr. 540 N. 48th
Irving, W. fr. 37th, ab. Spruce
Irwin, E. fr. 13th bel. Green
Isaac's ct., fr. 918 Vine
Isabella, fr. 2732 Emiline
Iserminger, fr. 1220 Budd
Islington la., N. E. fr. Ridge av.
ab. 25th
Ivanhoe, S. fr. Pewter. ab. 4th
Ivy. fr. 508 S. 10th
J. N. fr. Kensington, av., ab. I
Jacob pl., fr. 835 Randolph
Jacoby, fr. 1218 Monterey
Jacoby av., fr. 131 Oxford
Jackson, E. fr. Martha
Jackson, fr. 3414 N. 8th
Jackson, fr. 1021 Ellsworth
Jackson, E & W 2200 S
Jackson,fr. Washington,(Myk.)
Jackson, N. fr. Tucker, (Fyk.)

James, W. fr. Edgemont
James, W. fr. Orthodox, (Fkd.)
Jamison, fr. 1226 S. 7th
Jamison's ct., fr. 2331 Hamilton
Jane, fr. 717 Yhost
Janney, N. fr. Ann, ab. Tulip
Jarvis, E. fr. 4th, bel. Reed
Jasper, fr. 2301 N. Front
Java pl., S. fr. Vine, ab. 9th
Jay, N. fr. Wallace, ab. 8th
Jayne, W. fr. 34 S. 6th
Jefferson, W. fr. Johnson, Gtn.)
Jefferson. N. fr. Oxford, (Fkd.)
Jefferson, W. fr. Cresson,(Myk.)
Jefferson, E. & W. 1500 N
Jefferson pl., fr. 948 N. Front
Jeffrey pl., fr. 1108 N. Front
Jenning's ct.. fr. 120 Marion
Jenks, E. fr. Richmond, (Bdg.)
Jenkins, fr. 23 N. 2d
Jerusalem pl., fr. 1210 Pearl
Jessamine, fr. 927 S. 15th
Jessup, fr. 1115 Catharine
John ct., fr. 408 N. 24th
John, N. fr. Buckius, (Bdg.)
John, fr. Waln, (Fkd.)
John, fr. Cresson, (Myk.)
John, fr. 3520 Mascher
John's pl., fr. 1313 Wheat
Johnson, E. & W. 2800 S
Johnson, fr. Gtn., av. (Gtn.)
Johnson, N. fr. Sellers, (Fkd.)
Johnston, fr. 22 S. 20th
Joint al., fr. 21 S. 15th
Jones, fr. 20 N. 17th
Jordan, N. fr. Reed, ab. 20th
Jordan's pl., fr. 2415 Callowhill
Josephine, fr. Church, (Fkd.)
Joy, W. fr. 10th bel. Pine
Joyce, N. fr. Moore, ab. 4th
Joyce, S. fr.Venango,ab. Amber
Juan pl., E. fr. 13th, ab. South
Judd pl , fr. 749 Passyunk av
Judge,W. fr. Edgemont,ab.Ann
Judson, N. fr. Brown, ab. 23d
Julia, fr. 153 Fairmount av
Juliana, fr. 517 Vine
Julius pl., fr. 1007 S. 2d
June, S. fr. Seneca, ab. 47th
June, fr. 750 S. 7th
Juniata, N. fr. Reed, ab. 4th
Juniata av., E. & W., 4200 N.
Juniata, N. fr. Arch. ab. 62d
Justice, fr. 1220 S. 26th
Justice's ct., fr. 528 N. 2d
Juvenal,N. fr. Walnut, ab. 10th
K., fr. 3100 Kensington av.
Kane, N. fr. Darcy
Kane's ct., fr. 921 Rodman
Kane's pl., fr. 131 Carpenter
Kater, fr. 618 Lloyd
Kates, fr. 812 S. 15th
Kauffman, fr. 811 S. 4th
Kauffman ct., fr. 121 N. 2d
Keating pl., fr. 522 N. 2d
Keble, W. fr. 8th, bel. Pine
Keefe, fr. 1118 S. Front
Keeler's ln., fr. 1929 S. Front
Keichline's ct., fr. 1137 Charlotte
Keichline pl., N. fr. 1133 Olive
Kelly, W. fr. 13th, ab. Chestnut
Kelly's ct., fr. 317 German
Kelley's la., fr. Green la. (Myk)
Keenan's ct., fr. 1429 Gtn. av
Kelly s ct., fr. 237 Washigt'n av
Kelton, fr. 1416 Race
Kemble, fr. 416 S. 12th
Kempton, fr. 240 S. 5th
Kenilworth pl., fr. 3319 Emerald
Kennebec ct., fr. 2011 Naudian
Kennedy, fr. Tacony, (Fkd.)
Kennedy's ct., fr. 924 N. Front
Kenny pl., fr. 220 Monroe
Kensington av., N. fr. 2401 N. Front
Kent, W. fr. 22d, ab. Pine
Kenton pl., N. fr. Lodge
Kenwood pl., fr. 1015 Hamilton
Kenworthy's ct., fr. 727 Cherry
Kenyon, N. fr. New, ab. 2d
Keron pl., fr. 420 St. John
Kerr, fr. 930 Lawrence
Kerr, S. fr. Pine, ab. 22d
Kerr, fr. 829 N. 5th
Kershaw av., W. fr. Lancaster av., ab. 49th
Kershow, fr. 1434 Race
Kessler, fr. 921 Fairmount av
Kessler pl., fr. 341 Fairm't av
Kessly, fr. 560 N. 41st
Kettlewell, fr. 3430 Bath
Keturah pl., fr. 1015 St. John
Keyser, fr. 1327 N. 5th
Keyser, fr. Columbia, bel. Wildey
Keyser's ct., fr. 312 New Mkt.
Keyser's ct., fr. 920 N. 6th
Keyser's la., fr. Gtn. av.,(Gtn.)
Kiblen pl., fr. 123 Green
Kiehl, fr. 3114 Amber
Kildare, W. fr. Osprey
Kilpatrick's ct., fr. 609 Lomb'd
Kimball, fr. 1028 S. 19th
King's ct., fr. 2118 Sansom
King s ct., fr. 1321 Kates
Kingsessing av., S. W., fr. 41st and Woodland av
Kingston, fr. 3619 Richmond
Kingston, fr. 218 S. 13th
Kinley's ct., fr. 1626 Lombar
Kinsley's pl., fr. 253 N. 6th
Kirby pl., fr. 419 Garden
Kirk, N. fr. Gtn. av. (Gtn.)
Kirkbride, E. fr. School, (Bdg.)

Kirkham pl., fr. 718 Race
Kirkpatrick ct., fr. 719 S. 6th
Kips, S. f. Indiana, bel. Front
Kline's ct., fr. 928 N. 3d
Kline's row, fr. 1305 Lawrence
Kneass, E. fr. 417 N. 15th
Knickerbocker pl., fr. 1432 Cherry
Knight's ct., fr. 822 Cherry
Knowles' av., fr. 2418 Naudian
Knorr, N. E. fr. Fillmore
Knox, N. fr. Queen, (Gtn.)
Knox, N. fr. Brown, ab. 9th
Kressler pl., fr. 421 Norris
Krider's al., fr. 734 S. Front
Krider's ct., fr. 719 Alaska
Kurtz, N. fr. Poplar, ab. 11th
**Lancon pl.**, fr. Krider's al.
Lafayette, fr. 1156 S. 9th
Lafferty's ct., fr. 522 Christian
La Grange, fr. 32 N. 2d
La Harpe r l., fr. Rugan, ab. 4th
Lambert, W. fr. 13th, ab. Arch
Lanark pl., fr. 938 Beach
Lancaster, fr. 3220 Market
Lancaster, fr. 112 Marion
Lancaster av., fr. 3201 Market
Lancer's ct., fr. 1320 Passyunk av
Landis, W. fr. 238 S. 4th
Landreth, fr. 122 N. 12th
Lane's ct., fr. 1328 Lombard
Lansing pl., fr. 419 South
Lardner, fr. 118 S. 15th
Larkin, fr. 1121 South
Lathbury's ct., fr. 518 Alaska
Latimer, fr. 234 S. 15th
Latimer, fr. 1127 Otis
Latimer ct., fr. 223 Germa
Latimer pl., fr. 236 S. 17th
Latour's ct., fr. 816 Willow
Laurel, E. fr. 2d, ab. Poplar
Laurel, fr. 4833 Gtn. av. (Gtn.)
Laurens, fr. School, (Gtn.)
Lava pl., fr. 211 Duponceau
Lawrence, fr. 418 Brown
Law's ct., fr. 220 Christian
Lawson, fr. 1121 Pearl
Leadbeater's av., E. fr. Lybrand
Leaden's ct., fr. 724 Alaska
Lebanon, fr. 920 Fitzwater
Lafayette, N. fr. Wayne, (Gtn.)
La Grange, fr. 1324 Carpenter
Lambden, fr. Tasker, ab. 17th
Lambert, fr. Clearfield, ab. Bath
Lambert, S. fr. Berks, ab. 20th
Landing, fr. 2501 Green
Landsdown, fr. 5322 Lanc't av.
Langdon pl., 1308 Corn
Larkin, fr. 11 South
Lark, N. fr. William, ab. Tulip
Latona, fr. 1724 S. 16th
Latona, fr. 1523 N. 21st
Lawrence av., fr. 1318 S. 18th

Layman pl., fr. 725 Jayne
League, fr. 1026 S. 19th
Leamy, fr. 121 Lehigh av
Leander, fr. 1600 Mifflin
LeBrun, E. fr. Harvey, (Gtn.)
Ledger pl., fr. 34 N. 2d
Lefevre, E. fr. Fkd. cr., (Bdg.
Lee, fr. 21 Cumberland
Lee, W. fr. 18th, bel. Market
Leed's av., fr. 1406 Vine
Leed's pl., fr. 1220 Olive
Lee's pl., fr. 1018 Alaska
Lehigh av., E. & W. 2700 N
Lehman, S. fr. Green, (Gtn.)
Leiper's ct., fr. 41 N. 11th
Leib pl., E. fr. Annapolis
Leibert. fr. Robinson, (Myk.)
Leib, S. fr. Harrison
Leinan pl., fr. Harriet
Leiper, N. fr. Frankford, (Fkd.)
Leiper, E. fr. 19 S. 13th
Leiper pl., fr. 514 Marriott
Leisenring, fr. 228 N. 12th
Leithgow, fr. 417 Poplar
Lejee, fr. 918 Dauphin
Lemon, fr. 614 N. 16th
Lemon ct., fr. 1324 Fkd. av.
Lena, fr. Collom, (Gtn.)
Lentz, W. fr. 1218 S. 11th
Lentz's ct., fr. 1320 Passayunk
Leon, fr. 1000 Washington av
Leopard, fr. 17 Richmond
Lesher, N. fr. Orthodox, (Fkd.)
Letitia, fr. 119 Chestnut
Letitia ct., fr. 120 N. 23d
Letterly, fr. 2431 Kensington av
Levan pl., fr. 912 S. 9th
Levant, S. fr. Pear
Leverington av., (Myk.)
Levina, fr. 520 S. 3d
Levy's ct., N. fr. Trout
Lewellen's av., fr. 920 Beach
Lewis, W. fr. 1200 S. 36th
Lewis, N. fr. Tioga ab. Thompson
Lex, fr. 830 N. 15th
Lex, N. fr. Eadline, ab. 44th
Leyden's ct., fr. 221 N. 10th
Lib rty, N. fr. Myrtle, ab. 40th
Liberty, fr. Robinson, (Myk.)
Liberty, fr. 217 N. 10th
Library, W. fr. 4th, ab. Walnut
Lilly Ann, fr. 1018 Bainbridge
Lima pl., N. fr. South, ab. 6th
Lincoln av., fr. 724 Fallon
Linden, fr. Mulberry, (Fkd.)
Linden, S. fr. Green, ab. 9th
Linden, fr. 1231 Richmond
Linden pl., fr. 1824 Alaska
Linden pl. E. fr. Main, (Gtn.)
Lindsey, fr. 1620 Bainbridge
Lindsey av., fr. 1118 South
Lingo, fr. 1722 Carpenter

Linn, fr. 418 N. 22.1
Linnard, fr. 1330 S. 8th
Linney, E. fr. Gaul, ab. Tioga
Linton, W. fr. 20th, ab. Walnut
Linville, fr. 2416 Green
Linwood, W. fr. 48th, ab. Aspen
Linwood pl., fr. 12 N. 9th
Lippincott, fr. 3124 N. 6th
Lisbon, W. fr. Gilles al.
Lisle, fr. 814 Bainbridge
Lister pl., fr. 320 Bainbridge
Litchfield, fr. 122 Bainbridge
Litchfield pl., fr. Annapolis
Litford pl., fr. 66 Laurel
Little Ann pl., fr. 1338 Carpnt'r
Little Belt pl., fr. 919 S. 2d
Little Boy's ct., fr. 114 Arch
Little Medina, fr. 1328 S. 7th
Little Pine, N. fr. Warren
Little Summer, fr. 124 N. 22d
Little Wayne, fr. Lehman (Gtn)
Livingston, fr. 721 Gold
Lloyd, N. fr. 1411 Fitzwater
Lloyd, fr. 414 Serrell
Lock, W. fr. Penn, (Myk.)
Lock pl., fr. Leopard
Lockland pl., fr. 1321 Fairmount av
Locust, fr. Garden, (Bdg.)
Locust, fr. 228 S. 4th
Locust av., N. fr. Willow (Gtn)
Lodge, W. fr. 2d, ab. Walnut
Logan, fr. 3420 N. 21st
Logan square, fr. Race, ab. 18th
Lombard, E. & W., 500 S.
Lombard row, fr. 712 Lombard
Long, fr. 920 McKean
Long la., fr. 1910 Washngt'n av
Long's ct., fr. 748 S. 3d
Longfellow pl., fr. 1216 Bainbridge
Longstreth ct., fr. Levant
Loomis pl., fr. 2217 Shamokin
Lorain, N. fr. Green, ab. 7th
Lorain pl., fr. 1029 N. 4th
Loud pl., fr. 810 Enquirer
Loudon, E. & W., 4900 N.
Louisa av., fr. 107 Union
Louty pl., fr. 524 Christian
Lounden pl., fr. 321 N. 2d
Lowber, N. fr. Filbert, ab. 39th
Lowndes pl., fr. 321 N. 2d
Loxley pl., N. fr. Arch, ab. 3d
Loyel, E. fr. York, ab. Moyer
Lucus pl., fr. 1108 Gtn. av
Lucy, E fr. Almond, bel. York
Ludlow, fr. 22 S. 29th
Ludwig, fr. 4032 Haverford av.
Lukens, fr. 1112 S. 15th
Luther, fr. 955 St. John
Luzerne, E. & W., 4000 N.
Lybrand, N. fr. 1319 Race
Lydia, S. W. fr. Sites

Lydia, fr. 222 S. Juniper
Lydia, fr. 4615 Silverton av.
Lynch ct., fr. 762 S. 2d
Lynd, W. fr. 4th, ab. Green
Lyndall al., fr. 216 S. 12th
Lynn pl., fr. 819 St. John
McAfee's ct., fr. 510 South
McAllister's al., fr. 150 N. 8th
McAllister's ct., fr. 1120 Frankford av
McAlpin, S. fr. Walnut, ab. 36t'ı
McAnall's pl., fr. 2129 Spruce
McAnally's ct., fr. 735 Carpntr
McAtee's ct., fr. 1528 Cadwalader
McAlravy, fr. 1106 Milton
McCallum, W. fr. Mortan, (Gtn.)
McCann's ct., fr. 417 Christian
McCann's pl., fr. 425 Marriott
McCanns ct., fr. 831 St. Mary
McCartney's ct., fr. 814 Christian
McCaw's row, fr. 775 S. 3d
McClaskey's ct, fr. 522 S. 6th
McClean's ct. fr. 1111 Bainbridge
McCleary's ct., fr. 1528 Lombard
McClellan, fr. 1818 S. 2d
McClellen, S. fr. Vienna
McClure's ct., fr. 1520 Pearl
McCormick's av., fr. 129 N. 23d
McCoy's ct., fr. 926 S. 6th
McCrea, fr. 744 S. Juniper
McCristle's al., fr. 1336 Gtn., av
McCurdy, fr. 1130 S. 26th
McDavitt's ct., fr. 527 Marriott
McDavitt's ct., fr. 330 St. John
McDonald pl., 230 N. 15th
McDuffie, fr. 522 S. 18th
McFaddens ct., fr. 1014 South
McFadden pl., fr. 1532 Lombard
McFarland, W. fr. 42 bel. Aspen
McFarland ct., fr. 1621 Moravian
McFarran, fr. 3801 Gtn. av., (Gtn.)
McGaw's Row, fr. 775 S. 4th
McGinley's ct., fr. 515 Marriott
McGrath, fr. 841 Lawrence
McIllwain, fr. 1226 S. 3d
McIntire's ct., fr. 429 Christian
McKean, E. & W, 2000 S
McKeans ct., fr. 618 Locust
McKean's av., fr. Clapier, (Gtn.)
McKee's av., fr. 631 St. Mary
McKee's ct., fr. 1320 Lombard
McKnight's ct., fr. 1812 Naudain
McLean, fr. 123 Otter
McLaughlin's av., fr. Little Summer
McLaughlin's ct., fr. 428 Marriott
McManeman ct., E. fr. Sycamore
McManemy's ct., fr. 428 German
McManus, fr. 2143 Gtn. av.
McMutten's ct., fr. 424 Walnut

McNally, fr. 2315 Biddle
McNickle's pl.,fr. 828 Carpenter
McPherson's ct., fr. 2230 Hamilton
McWilliams av., fr. 106 Thompson
Mackey, fr. 1324 S. 2d
Mackinaw, fr. 234 N. 8th
Mackham, fr. 724 N. 17th
Macleod pl., fr. 418 Race
Maddox pl., fr. 729 S. 4th
Madison, N. fr. Race, ab. 11th
Madison av., fr, 3228 Emerald
Madison ct., fr. 637 St. Mary
Madison sqr., fr. 828 S. 22d
Magilton's ct., N. fr. Kates
Magnet, S. fr. Green la., (Myk.)
Magnolia, N, fr. Willow ab. 5th
Magnolia, E. fr. Haines, (Gtn)
Maiden, fr. Letcher, (Myk.)
Maiden la.,fr.Lanc'r av. ab. 50th
Main, fr. Rittenhouse, (Myk.)
Maison pl., fr. 1318 Silver
Malcolm pl., fr. 1831 Gtn., av
Manayunk av., (Myk.)
Manderson, fr. 1016 Beach
Mangrove pl., fr. 626 South
Manhatten pl., fr. 1015 Hamilton
Manheim,fr. 4552 Gtn av.,(Gtn.)
Manley, fr. 1721 Ridge av.
Manilla, fr. 924 S. 9th
Mannekin, fr. 517 Norris
Manning, W. fr. 22d ab. Spruce
Mann's ct., fr. 928 Hamilton
Manor, S. E. fr. Adams, (Myk.)
Manor, S. fr. Berks, ab. 4th
Manor pl., S. fr. Poplar, ab. 3d
Mansfield pl., fr. 540 N. Front
Manship, fr. 142 Norris
Manship, fr. 1124 Locust
Mansine pl., fr. 924 Melon
Manton, fr. 1224 S. 17th
Maplewood, N. fr. Wyne, (Gtn.)
Maple, W. fr. 8th, ab. Race
Marble, fr. 18 S. 10th
Marble ct., 8. fr. Marble,
Margaret, fr. Trenton av., (Fkd.)
Margaretta, fr. 419 N. 2d.
Margaretta, fr. 622 Wharton
Margaretta pl.,fr.117 Margaretta
Maria, fr. 718 N. 4th
Mariner, fr. 1018 S. 13th
Marion, fr. 1122 S. Front
Marion pl., fr. 518 Christian
Marion, W. fr. Lehman, (Gtn.)
Marker, fr. 1626 S. 2d
Market, W. fr. Delaware av., No. 1 N. & S.
Market al., fr. 429 N. 16th
Markham, fr. 722 N. 17th
Markle pl., fr. 519 S. 2d
Markley pl., fr. 130 Spruce
Markoe, fr. 4623 Silverton av.
Mark's la., W. fr. 11th, ab. Arch
Marlborough, fr. 1521 Fkd av
Marley's ct., fr. 1822 Ann
Marmion pl., fr. 228 Christian
Marmora, fr. 728 Beach
Marshall ct., fr. Campbell
Marshall, N. fr. Vine, ab. 6th
Marsden pl.,fr.1528 Cadwalader
Marseilles pl., fr. 525 N. 15th
Marston. N. fr. Budden's al.
Marston, fr. 2715 Jefferson
Martindale pl., fr. 1428 Spring Garden
Martin, fr. 1827 Catherine
Martin's ct., fr. 921 St. John
Martin's al., fr. 224 S. Dela. av.
Marten, E. fr. Peachem, (Myk.)
Martha, fr. 340 E. Lehigh av.
Martin ct., fr. 218 Carpenter
Martin pl., fr. 2123 Vine
Mary, fr. 1326 Thompson
Mary, fr. 927 S. 2d
Mary, fr. 1214 S. 7th
Mary, fr. Allen, ab. 40th
Marriott, fr. 925 S. 9th
Mascher, fr. 122 Girard av.
Master, E. & W., 1400 N.
Mater, N. fr. Ontario, ab. 15th
Matlack, fr. 1925 Parrish
Matamoras, fr. 1115 St. John
Matzinger's ct., fr. Landreth
Mattis, fr. 341 S. 2d
Mattson pl., S. fr. Crease
Maurice, fr. 1120 Passyunk av.
Maxwell's ct.. fr. 228 Christian
Maxwell's ct., fr. 1217 Alaska
May pl., fr. 1728 Lombard
May, W. fr. 748 S. 7th
May, fr. 4721 Westminster av.
Mayer's ct., fr. 245 N. 15th
Mayland, N. fr. Race, ab. 5th
Maynard pl., fr. Relief
Mead, 741 S. 2d
Meadow, E. fr. Paul, (Fkd.)
Meadow, N. fr. Bridge, (Bdg.)
Mechanic, fr. 520 Carpenter
Mechanic, fr. Morton, (Gtn.)
Mechanic, N. E. fr. Main, (Myk)
Meclaud pl., fr. 429 Monroe
Medical, fr. 124 S. 10th
Medina, W. fr. 7th, ab. Reed
Megary, fr. 128 E. Girard av.
Mehl, W. fr. Clinton, (Gtn.)
Melcher,fr.526 Susquehanna av
Melina pl., fr. 424 Gaskill
Melloy, fr. 26 S. 15th
Melon, W. fr. 9th, ab. Green
Melrose, W. fr. 57th, ab. Vine
Melrose, N. fr. Frankford (Fkd)
Melvale, fr. 1220 William
Melville pl., fr. 124 Spruce
Memhoelzler's ct., fr. 711 Brook

Memphis, N.fr.Vienna,ab.Gaul
Mendon pl., fr. 420 N. 5th
Meninge's ct., fr. 1326 Passay'k
Mercer, fr. 2024 S. 5th
Mercer, fr. Jefferson, (Gtn.)
Merchant, fr. 12 S. 4th
Mercury, fr. 329 E.Montgomery
Mercy, fr. 2016 S. 10th
Mercer, N. fr. Jefferson, (Gtn.)
Mercer, N. fr. Gold
Meredith, fr. 728 N. 23d
Merida pl., fr. 719 S. Front
Merritt, W. fr. Swanson
Merino, fr. 1130 N. 2d
Mermaid la., E. fr. Gtn.av (Gtn)
Merrick, S. fr. 1420 Filbert
Mervine, fr. 1121 Stiles
Mervine pl., fr. 1424 Mervine
Metcalf, fr. Shirker's al
Mechan, S. fr. Chew, (Gtn.)
Meehan, N. fr. Morris, ab. 11th
Meetler, E. fr. 7th, ab. Berks
Mica, N. fr. Seneca, ab. 47th
Middle al., W. fr. 6th, ab. Pine
Middleton, fr. 2028 Tulip
Middleton's ct., fr. 418 Dillwyn
Mifflin, E. & W., 1900 S.
Mifflin, E. fr. Ridge av. (Myk.)
Milburn, fr. 2.0 S. 12th
Mildred, S. fr. McKean, ab. 8th
Mildenhall, fr. 1720 Jackson
Miles, W. fr. 10th, ab. Spruce
Milford, fr. 224 N. 23d
Mill, fr. 4779 Gtn. av. (Gtn.)
Mill, E. fr. Frankford, (Fkd.)
M ller, fr. 822 Washington av
Miller, fr. 3912 Lancaster av
Miller. fr. 5660 Gtn. av (Gtn.)
Miller's ct., fr. 1932 Belgrade
Millicent al., fr. 321 New Mkt.
Milligan's ct., fr. 1618 Lombard
Mills, fr. 820 Charlotte
Milman fr.920 Moyamensing av
Milton, fr. 930 S. 10th
Mineral pl., fr. 121 N. Broad
Mineral pl., fr. 122 Bread
Mineral, fr. 546 N. 13to
Minerva, fr. 538 N. 7th
Minor, fr. 28 S. 5th
M nster, fr. 820 S. 7th
Mint ct W fr H tton pl
Mintzer, fr 3.8 Brown
Mitchell, fr. Green la. (Myk.)
Moffett, N. fr. Ontario ab.Tulip
Moland av., fr. 521 N. 13th
Mole, fr. 1518 Wharton
Moliere's ct., fr. 208 Bainbridge
Monckton pl., fr. 1115 Vine
Monmouth, fr. 290 Gaul
Monroe, fr. 728 S. 2d
Montana, fr. 5628 Vine
Montcalm, fr. 1010 Fitzwater
Montgomery av. E.&W. 1800 N.

Montrose, fr. 924 S. 16th
Monument, fr. 1928 N. 17h
Moore, E. & W., 1800 S.
Moore, fr. 731 S. 15th
Moore, W. fr. Amber, ab. Otis
Moore's av., fr. 730 N. Front
Moore's ct., fr. 1223 Alaska
Moravian, fr. 214 S. Broad
Morencia pl., fr. 968 Leithgow
Morgan, fr. 234 N. 9th
Morgan al., N. fr. Vine, ab. 2d
Moro, S. fr. Brinton, ab. 12th
Morris, fr. 1229 S. 2d
Morris, E. & W., 1700 S.
Morris, N. fr. Clapier. (Gtn.)
Morris ct , W. fr. Latitia
Morse, fr. 1834 N. 31st
Morses ct., fr. 1019 Nectarine
Morton, E. fr. Girard av. ab.Ash
Morton, W. fr. Centre, (Gtn.)
Morton av., fr. 315 Queen
Mosely, fr. 1428 S. 12th
Moss, W. fr. Charles
Moss Rose pl., fr. 220 Queen
Mott, fr. 1022 S. 13th
Moulder pl., fr. 519 Vincent
Mountain, W. fr. 8th, ab.Morris
Mount Airy la. (Gtn.)
Mount Holly, fr. 1714 Wharton
Mount Pleasant, fr. 1236 Taney
Mount Pleasant fr.Gtn.av(Gtn.)
Mount Vernon, fr. 624 N. 9th
Mousely pl., fr. 1533 Gtn. av
Moyer, fr. 319 E. Columbia
Moyer's al., fr. Main, (Myk.)
M yamensing av., fr. 901 S. 2d
Mulberry, fr. Harrison, (Fkd.)
Mulberry, N. fr. Baker, (Myk.)
Mulberry al., W. fr. 220 N. 5th
Mullen's ct., fr. 814 Essex
Mulford, fr. Ashton
Mulholland ct., fr. Barley
Mullen, fr. 319 Somerset
Muller, fr. 2613 Christian
Mulloney, fr. 229 S. 21st
Munson's ct , fr. 728 S. 4th
Muren's pl., fr. 720 Cherry
Murgitroyde pl., 220 S. 15th
Murray, fr. 234 S. 20th
Murray's ct., W. fr. Osprey
Murray's ct , S. fr. Sheaf's al.
Murray's ct., fr. 628 Bainbridge
Murray's ct., fr. 748 S. Front
Murphy ct., fr. 621 Bainbridge
Musgrave, fr. 1820 S. 31st
Musgrove, fr. Gorgas, (Gtn.)
Mustin ct., E. fr. Elder
Mutter, N. fr. York, bel. 2d
Muttonchop, fr. Oldham ct
Myer's av., fr. 242 S. 6th
Myer's ct., fr. 219 N. 15th
Myrtle, W. fr. 11th, ab. Parrish
Myrtle, W. fr. 39th, ab. Oregon

Myrtle, N. fr. Linden
**Nagle**, N. fr. Stiles, ab. 11th
Nahant, fr. 729 St. John
Narcissus pl., fr. 326 N. 8th
Nassau, W. fr. 21st & Ridge av.
Nassau, fr. 140 N. 9th
Nassau, fr. 2831 Tulip
Native, fr. 922 S. 5th
Natrona, fr. 3225 Oxford
Napa, fr. 3113 Reed
Nash, W. fr. Church, (Gtn )
Naudain, fr. 518 S. 18th
Navy, fr, 1322 S. Front
Naylor, fr. 1232 S. 11th
Nectarine, fr. 520 N. 8th
Neff, E. fr. Gaul, ab. Ann
Nellie's ct., fr. 218 N. 22d
Nelson, N. fr. Norris,bel.Moyer
Nelson, fr. 20 N 40th
Nelson's al.. fr. 413 St. John
Nelson's ct.. fr. 718 Lloyd
Neuit's ct., fr. 821 N. 4th
Neville pl., fr. Vine, ab. 5th
Nevin pl., fr. 1319 Carlton
New, E. fr. 4th, ab. Race
New, fr. Gtn av. (Gtn.)
Newbold, fr. 1923 Callowhill
Newbold, fr. 1418 Moore
Newkirk, fr. 531 E.Cumberland
Newkirk, fr. 2922 Brown
New Market, fr. 121 Vine
New Market pl., fr. 317 New
Newport, fr. Moore, ab. 33d
Newton, fr. 324 Carpenter
Niblo pl., fr. 1424 Spring Garden
Nice, N. fr. McFarran, (Gtn.)
Nicetown la., fr. 3410 Cambria
Nicholas, fr. 1630 N. 20th.
Nicholson, fr. 618 Race
Nickel pl., fr. 729 S. Front
Nigley's ct., fr, 1526 Cadwallader
Ninevah pl., fr. 418 German
Nisbet pl., fr. 748 S. Front
Noble, E. & W., 500 N.
Nolan's av., fr. 1421 Parrish
Nonnater's ct., fr. 1020 Arch
Norfolk, fr. 850 Swanson
Norfolk, fr. 1428 Spruce
Norris, E. & W., 2000 N.
Norris, fr. McKean av. (Gtn.)
Norris pl., fr. 327 New Market
North, fr. 24 N. 5th
North, fr. 6 4 N. Broad
Northampton ct., fr. 428 Dillwyn
N. College av., fr. 1332 N. 20th
Northeast av,, fr. Marlborough
Norton, S. fr. Jefferson, (Gtn.)
Norwood, fr, 2125 Columbia av.
Norwood av., fr. 1917 Cambria
Nugent's ct:, fr. 726 Bainbridge
Oak, W. fr. Baker, (Myk.)

Oakford, fr. 1218 S. Broad
Oakford pl., fr. 222 Gaskill
Oakland, fr. Sellers, (Fkd.)
Oat, fr. 1133 Sheaff
Ocean, fr. 118 Dana
Oddfellows' av., fr. 313 Brown
Ogden, fr. 824 N. 9th
O'harra's ct., fr. 724 S. 7th
Ohio, fr. 423 S. 12th
Oldham ct., fr. 819 St. John
Olive, fr. 728 N. 10th
Olive ct., fr. 1316 Olive
Oliver, fr. 930 S. 10th
Olivet pl., fr. 1728 Lombard
Olivia, fr. 3628 Myrtle
Olivia pl.. fr. 1522 Cadwallader
Onas, fr. 732 N. Front
One, fr. 1726 Mifflin
O'Neal, fr. 1106 Howard
Oneida pl., fr. 819 New Market
O'Neil's ct., fr. 1624 Lombard
Ony, fr. Ash, (Bdg )
Ontario, fr. 1329 Parrish
Opal, N. fr. Jefferson, ab. 19th
Orange, fr. 238 S. 7th
Orchard, fr. 419 Rawle
Orchard, N. fr. Mill, (Fkd.)
Oregon, E. & W., 2700 S.
Oregon, W. fr.39th, ab. Aspen
O'Hara's al., fr. 919 South
Orion, fr. 3420 Eadline
Orion, W. fr. 3d, ab. Market
Orkney, fr. 417 Norris
Orleans, fr. 2728 Frankford av.
Orleans, S. fr. 1622 Mifflin
Ormes, N. fr. Tuscuram
Orr, N. fr. 1617 Francis
Orrianna, fr. 329 Diamond
Orr's ct., fr. 1321 Rodman
Orthodox, E. fr. Leiper, (Fkd.)
Osage av., fr. 420 S. 4th
Osage av., fr. Heath, ab. 12th
Osbeck pl., W. fr. Jay
Osborne's ct., fr. Duponceau
Oscar, fr. 3021 Gray's Ferry rd.
Osceola, W. fr. Herman, (Gtn.)
Osler av., N. fr. Noble, ab. 5th
Osprey, N. fr. Biddle, ab. 24th
Otis, fr. 2201 N. Front
Otsego, fr. 26 Christian
Otsego, pl., fr. 124 Prime
Outlet, W. fr. 21st, ab. Green
Otter, E. fr. 1145 N. 2d
Ovington, S. fr. South, ab. 8th
Owen, fr. 1230 S. 5th
Owen, E. fr. McNally
Oxford, E. & W. 1600 N.
Oxford, fr. Frankford. (Fkd.)
**Pacific**, fr. 1424 Susquehanna av
Pacific, fr. 3618 N. 17th
Packer, E. & W., 3100 S.
Packer pl., N. fr. Craven

Page, W. fr. 16th, ab. Norris
Pagoda, fr. Earl, ab. 24th
Palethrop, fr. 145 Girard av.
Palisade pl., N. fr. Quarry
Pallas, fr. 1229 Morris
Palm, N. fr. Gilbert, ab 9th
Palmer, W. fr. Beach, ab. Elm
Palmer's ct., fr. 330 S. 4th
Palmetto, fr. 230 N. 15th
Palo Alto, S. fr. Pine, ab. 20th
Panama av. fr. 262 S. 20th
Paradise al., fr. 414 Market
Parade, fr. 1218 S. 12th
Park, S. fr. Federal, ab. 27th
Park, fr. 1830 Fitzwater
Park, fr. 3124 N. 19th
Park av., fr. 2100 N. Broad
Park av. fr. 1327 Jefferson
Parker, fr. 518 Carpenter
Parkham, fr. 741 S. Front
Parrish, W. fr. 5th ab. Brown
Pascal, fr. 1014 S. 10th
Paschal, fr. 4924 Lancaster av.
Passyunk av., fr. 432 South
Pastorius, fr. Gtn. av., (Gtn.)
Path, N. fr. Race, ab. 15th
Patterson's ct., fr. 1327 Naudain
Patton, fr. 3129 Reed
Patton, fr. Coulter, (Gtn.)
Patton's al., fr. 1624 Lombard
Patton's ct., fr. 732 Alaska
Paul, fr. 1022 S. 6th
Paul, fr. Frankford, (Fkd.)
Paxton, fr. 1118 S. 5th
Paynter's ct., fr. 419 German
Peach, fr. 121 Green
Peach, fr. 4920 Paschall
Peacham, fr. Green la., (Myk.)
Pear, E. fr. 3d, ab. Spruce
Pear, fr. 3521 Silverton av.
Pear, fr. Mulberry, (Fkd.)
Pear, S. E. fr. Peach, (W. P.)
Pearl, W. fr. 10th, ab. Vine
Pearl, fr. Mechanic. (Myk.)
Pearl al., fr. Prosperous al,
Peale, fr. Mill, (Gtn.)
Pedan's av., fr. 1826 Naudain
Peel, S. fr. Vanhorn
Pegg, E. fr. 420 N. 2d
Pegg al., S. fr. Pegg
Pemberton, fr. 730 S. 18th
Pemberton, fr. 1322 Wallace
Pembroke, S. fr. 1320 Dauphin
Pembroke, fr. 524 Noble
Pembroke pl., fr. 214 N. 2d
Penn, fr. Lefevre, (Bdg.)
Pendinnis pl., fr. 555 Charlotte
Penn, S. fr. Chew, (Gtn.)
Penn, S. fr. 14 Pine
Penn, N. fr. 4169 Main, (Myk.)
Penn. N. fr. Pine, (Fkd.)
Penn al., fr. 320 St. John
Pennel's ct., fr. Rose

Pennington, fr. 226 Marriott
Pennsgrove, fr. 829 41st
Pennock, fr. 2719 Hare
Pennsylvania av., fr. 506 N. Broad
Pennsylvania av., fr. 518 Vine
Penrose, fr. 1812 Jackson
Pensive pl., fr. 1120 Wood
Pepper, fr. 2630 Cedar
Pequinot pl., fr. 831 St. John
Percy, fr. 917 Poplar
Percy pl., 417 German
Perkenpine's ct., fr. 729 New Market
Perkiomen, fr. 1719 Francis
Perry, N. fr. Race, ab. 13th
Perth, N. fr. Parrish, ab. 7th
Peter's fr. 1118 S. 12th
Peter's al., fr. 820 Charlotte
Petroleum, fr. 123 Walnut
Petty, E. fr. Bath, ab. Russell
Pharo, fr. 1823 Catharine
Phillellena, fr. Gtn. av., (Gtn.)
Philip, N. fr. Master, ab. 2d
Philadelphia, fr. 1529 Park av
Physick la., fr. Gtn. av., (Gtn.)
Pierce, W. fr. 4th, ab. Moore
Pierce, fr. Frankford cr. (Fkd.)
Pincus ct., fr 625 Marshall
Pine, E. & W., 400 S.
Pine, fr. 4326 Fkd. av., (Fkd.)
Pike, E. & W., 3900 N.
Pike, N. fr. Cherry, ab. 12th
Pilling, fr. Pine, (Fkd.)
Pine Tree, fr. 222 Willow
Pink, N. fr. Master, ab. 3d
Piper's ct., fr. 617 St. John
Placid pl., fr. 842 S. 2d
Plane, fr. 1328 Lancaster
Pleasant, fr. 5537 Gtn. av., (Gtn.)
Pleasant, fr. Mechanic, (Myk.)
Pleasant Retreat, fr. 634 N. 7th
Pleasant row, fr. 2014 Spruce
Pleffenburg pl. fr. 835 Cherry
Pleice's ct., fr. 330 Garden
Plover, fr. 1136 S. 7th
Plum, E. fr Richmond, ab. Ash
Plumb, S. fr. Mulberry, (Fkd.)
Plumstead pl., fr 1920 Sansom
Plymouth, fr. 220 S. 19th
Plynlimmon pl., fr. 224 N. Front
Pollard, E. fr. Canal, ab. Front
Pollock, E. & W. 3000 S.
Pollock's ct. fr. 1614 Lombard
Poplar, E & W., 900 N.
Poplar E. fr Green la., (Myk.)
Porcelain fr 19th, 131 S.
Porter, E. & W., 2500 S.
Porter's ct., fr. 331 St. John
Portland, fr. 420 N. 11th
Potts, fr. 670 N. 12th
Poulson, N. fr. Spruce, ab. 25th

Poulson, fr. 1840 S. 2d
Powder Mill la,fr.Leiper,(Fkd)
Powell, W. fr. 5th, ab. Pine
Powelton av , W. fr. 224 N. 32d
Pratt, N. fr. Melrose, (Bdg )
Presbyterian la., (Gtn.)
Prescott pl., fr. 1227 Hamilton
Preston, fr. 4031 Eadline
Preston, fr. 929 Wallace
Price. fr. 2331 Jasper
Price, N. fr. Gtn. av. (Gtn )
Price's ct., fr. 1132 Rodman
Price's ct., fr. 1115 Bainbridge
Price's ct., fr. 304 Lombard
Pricilla, N. fr. Soutn, ab. 4th
Prime, fr. 1129 S. 3d
Princeton pl., fr. 1225 Irwin
Pritchett, fr. 1240 S. 13th
Prospect, fr 923 Thompson
Prosperous al., fr. 1110 Locust
Providence ct., fr. Sargeant
Pryor's ct., fr. 229 S. 10th
Pulaski av, E.fr. Franklin.(Gtn.)
Putnam, E. fr. 2d, ab. Oxford
Prune, N. fr. Orthodox, (Fkd.)
**Quarry**, W. fr. 2d, ab. Arch
Quarry ct., fr. 2533 Callowhill
Queen, fr. 823 S. 6th
Queen, S. fr. Gtn. av., (Gtn.)
Queen av., S. fr. Queen, ab. 3d
Queen's ct., fr. 927 Federal
Queen's ct., fr. 842 Lawrence
Quiggs ct , fr. 2024 Beach
Quigg's ct., fr. 9 Vine
Quigley's ct., fr. 614 Charles
Quincey, fr. Carpenter, (Gtn.)
Quince, S. fr. Walnut, ab. 11th
**Race**, E. & W., 200 N
Rachel, N. fr. Brown, bel. 2d
Rachel's row, fr. 431 Dillwyn
Railroad, fr. Norris, bel. Front
Rainbow, W. fr. Blair, bel. Otis
Ralston. fr. 417 S. Juniper
Randall's ct., fr. 240 Duponceau
Randolph, fr. 2746 Memphis
Randolph, N. fr. Brown, ab.5th
Randolph av. fr. 724 Race
Ransom pl., fr. 231 N. 5th
Ranstead pl., fr. 40 S. 4th
Raspberry, fr. 920 Walnut
Ratcliffe, fr. Lombard, ab. 7th
Rau's ct., fr. 1530 Lackawana
Rawle, E. fr. 5th, ab. Brown
Ray's av., fr. 18 Marston
Reading av.fr.2722 Delaware av
Rebecca, fr. Haverford ab. 40th
Reckless, fr. 929 S. Front
Redner, fr. 1523 N. 22d
Redwood, fr. 1234 S. 3d
Reed, E. & W. 1400 S.
Reese. S. fr. York, ab. 5th
Reeves, W. fr. 20th, ab. Vine
Register pl., fr. 1215 Catherine

Reid's av., fr. 718 Fallon
Reiff's av., fr. 1234 N. Front
Reimer's av. fr. 1129 Poplar
Relief, fr. 1121 S. 2d
Rementer al., fr. 21 N. 10th
Rentscheler, fr. Melon, ab 11th.
Rennard, fr. 816 Wharton
Rex, W. fr. Gtn. av., (Gtn.)
Reynolds, fr. Richmond,(Bdg.)
Reynolds, fr. 820 Wharton
Rhodes, fr. 414 N. 18th
Richard, W. fr. 16th, bel. Pine
Richard, fr. 210 George
Richardson, fr. 1528 Ellsworth
Richardson's et., fr. 421 Race
Richland pl., fr. 144 Elfreth
Richmond, fr. Front, ab.Laurel.
Rickard's ct., fr. 231 George
Ridge, W. fr. Leiper, (Fkd.)
Ridge av., fr. 9th and Vine
Ridgeway, fr. 3419 Powlton av.
Ridgeway's ct., fr. 907 Torr
Ridley av., fr. Berks, bel. Gaul
Rigg's, fr. 829 Muller
Rigler's ct.,fr.1129 Frankford av
Rihl, fr. Palmer, ab. Belgrade
Riley, fr. Ridge av., (Myk )
Rinder pl., fr. 6 8 Marriott
Ringold, N. fr. Hare, ab. 24th
Ringold pl., fr. 422 S. 19th
Rio Grand pl, fr 1121 Moya'g av
Ripton pl., W. fr. 3d, ab. Poplar
Ristine fr. 810 Maple
Ritchie- .S. Fitzwater, ab, 13th.
Ritmeyer's ct., fr. 223 S. 2d
Ritner, E. & W., 2400 S.
Rittenhouse, fr, 228 S. 17th
Rittenhouse, fr. Gtn. av. (Gtn.)
Ritter, N. fr. Norris, ab. Gaul
Roach ct., S. fr. Savery
Robeson, N. fr. Gtn. av. (Gtn.)
Roberts av., fr. Gtn. av. (Gtn.)
Robeson's ct., fr. 1626 Lombard
Robeson's ct., fr. 918 N. Del. av
Robin, W. fr. 39th, bel. Pine
Robinson, fr. Main, (Myk.)
Robinson's al., fr. 632 Lombard
Rock, fr. 331 N. 16th
Rockford, fr. 440 N. 19th
Rockdale pl., fr. 627 Lombard
Rockhill pl., fr. Gtn. av. bel. 2d
Rockland, E. & W 5000 N.
Rockland, fr. 434 N. 35th
Rodman, W. fr. 9th, ab. South
Rodney, W. fr. 18th, ab. Pine
Rogers' ct., N. fr. Pegg
Ronaldson, fr. 918 South
Roney's ct., fr. 930 St. John
Rorrer, N. fr. Cambria, ab. D.
Rose, fr. 718 S. 13th
Rose, fr. 2421 Almond
Rose al., N. fr. Locust, ab. 10th
Rosehill,fr.Somerset,ab.Leamy

Roset, S. fr. Manheim, (Gtn.)
Ross, W. fr. Penn (Gtn.)
Ross, fr. 1428 Richmond
Ross av., fr. 523 S. 23d
Rough & Ready, fr. 207 Amber
Rowland's ct., fr. 712 Filbert
Roxborough, E. & W. 4100 N.
Royal, fr. 4611 Gtn. av., (Gtn.)
Ruan. W. fr. Paul, (Fkd.)
Rubicam pl., fr. 921 Noble
Rubicam, E fr Wister, (Gtn.)
Rudolph's av., fr. 739 Race
Rugan, S. fr. Noble, ab. 9th
Rule,W. fr. Lancaster,bel. Reed
Rule pl., fr. 729 S. 5th
Rundle, fr. 16th, bel. Lombard
Rupert, W. fr. 3d, bel. Green
Rush, fr. 2829 Frankford av.
Rush, W. fr. 20th, ab. Indiana
Russell, fr. 826 Bainbridge
Russell av., fr. 1529 Parrish
Ruth, fr. Hart's la., ab. Stouton
Rutler's ct., fr. 221 Federal
Ryan's ct., fr. 420 Christian
Ryan's pl., fr. 416 Christian
Rye, S. fr. Marion, ab. 2d
Ryle, S. fr. Palmer
**Sabine** pl., S. fr.Stanley, ab.3d
Sabula pl., fr. 811 Mackinaw
Sacramento av., S. fr. Day
Saffin pl, S fr. Ogden, ab. 9th
Salem al., fr. 1231 S. 12th
Salmon, N. fr. York, ab. Moyer
Salter, fr. 930 S. 7th
Samper pl., fr. 1023 S. 5th
Sanders' ct., fr. 1027 St. John
Sanderson, fr. 1226 S. 15th
Sansom, W. fr. 6th, ab. Walnut
Sarah, S. fr. Wildey
Saranak, W. fr. Rye, bel. Reed
Sargent pl, fr. 2518 Fkd. av.
Sargeant, W. fr. 9th, av. Race
Sa tain, N. fr. Poplar, ab. 11th
Sauer av., 1413 Randolph
Saunders N.fr.Filbert, ab. 38th
Savannah ct., fr. 1921 Beach
Savery, W. fr. Wildey
Saxon pl., S. fr. Stanley
Saxon, fr. 3114 Bath
Say, fr. 533 Bainbridge
Saybolt's ct., fr. 213 Noble
Scarrett's ct., fr. 705 Minster
Scattergood, fr. James, (Bdg.)
Scheaff's a ., fr. 228 N. 11th
S hell, S. fr. Vine ab. 8th
Schofield's ct., fr. 2008 Lombard
School, S. fr. 4800 Gtn. av., (Gtn)
Schaller, E. fr. Haines, (Gtn.)
Schallenger, N. fr. Serrill
Schleishmans al., E. fr. Canal
School, N. fr. Ash, (Bdg.)
Schoolhouse row,3419 Chestnut
Schryer's ct., fr. 820 Willow
Schuyler av , (Gtn.)
Sciota fr. 849 N, 45th
Scipio pl., fr. 45 N. 7th
Scott, W. fr. 19th, ab., Tasker
Scott's la,, fr. 3 21 Ridge av
Scranton pl., fr, 624 Filbert
Sears, fr. 1320 S, 6th
Second, fr. 24 N. 23d
Sedgley av., fr. 3201 Oxford
Sedgwick, fr. 615 Walnut
Seiser's ct., E. fr. Broad
Selfridge, fr. 1716 Bainbridge
Selfridge pl.,fr.1119 Bainbri lge
Sellers, N. fr. Adams, (Fkd.)
Sellers' ct., fr. 1315 Carlton
Sellers' ct., fr. 1416 Race
Seltzer, fr. 2714 N. Front
Senate, fr. 729 S. 2d
Seneca, W. fr. 43d, ab, Oregon
Seneca ct., W. fr. Belrose
Senneff, fr. 108 S. 23d
Senneff av., W. fr. Andres
Sepviva, N. fr 320 E. Berks
Serrill, fr. 2518 Almond
Serrill, fr. 1521 N Broad
Seubert's ct., E. fr. 1617 Gtn. av.
Seville, N. fr. Queen, ab. 2d
Sevier, E. fr. Manham, (Gtn.)
Seville, E. fr. Cresson, (Myk.)
Seybert, fr. 1534 N. 15th
Seymour, fr. Pulaski av. (Gtn.)
Shackamaxon, fr. 1301 Frank-
ford av.
Shaefer's ct., S. fr. Rawle
Shamokin, fr. 424 N. 22d
Sharkley's al., fr. 1216 Alaska
Sharpneck, E. fr. Gtn. av. (Gtn.)
Sharp's av., S fr. Canby
Sharswood, E.fr.24th,ab.Master
Shelburne av., fr. 421 Cherry
Sheldon pl., fr. 928 S Front
Shelly,fr. Clearfield,bel.Myrtle
Shellbark, fr. 146 N. 13th
Sheridan, S. fr. Berks, ab. 6th
Sherman, W. fr. Kirk, (Gtn.)
Shern's ct , fr. 1330 N. 2d
Shield's ct., S. fr. Relief
Shield's ct., fr., 1229 Catherin
Shiller, fr. 3421 N. 11th
Shirker's av., W. fr. Fawn
Shirker's al , fr. 520 Alaska
Shirker's ct., fr. 1212 Alaska
Shirley, fr. 719 N. 19th
Shiveley's av., fr. 811 Duane
Shock, fr. 2023 Market
Shock, fr. 15 Mead
Showaker, 2640 N. 22d
Shoemaker, fr. 23 S. 8th
Shoemaker ct., fr. 728 St. John
Shoemaker's al.,fr.Main,(Myk.)
Shoemaker's la., (Gtn.)
Short ct., E. fr. 12th, ab. Race
Shotwell's av.,fr.1221 Lawrence

Shur's la., fr. Main (Myk.)
Shunk. E. & W. 2600 S.
Sidmouth, N. fr. Cope's al.
Sidmouth pl., fr. 1810 Spruce
Sidney, fr. 812 Ellsworth
Siegel, fr. 1826 S. Front
Siegal, W. fr. 6th, ab. Mifflin
Silbert, N. fr. Reed, ab. 10th
Sillimen, N. fr. Eadline, ab. 43d
Silma pl., fr. 1920 Hamilton
Siloam, N. fr. Otis, ab. Almond
Silver, fr. 23 N. 12th
Silver, fr. 2724 Leamy
Silver's ct., fr. 430 Walnut
Silverton av., fr. 400 N. 32d
Silvia pl., S. fr. Poplar, ab. 3d
Simes, fr. 24 S. 22d
Simes' ct., fr. 621 Lombard
Simpson's ct., fr. 122 Catherine
Simpson's ct., fr. 926 S. Front
Singler's row, fr. 1212 N. 2d
Siner, fr. 22d, ab. Reed
Sisty, fr. 917 Montgomery av.
Sites, fr. 119 Otter
Sixth av., fr. 1320 Randolph
Skerritt's ct., S. fr. Aurora
Skill's pl., fr. 820 S. 3d
Sloan, fr. 3931 Filbert
Smaltz av., fr. 1529 Cabot
Smedley, S. fr. Erie, ab. 6th
Smethurst pl., fr. 431 N. 24th
Smith's ct., fr. 1128 Lombard
Smith's ct., fr. 1630 Philip
Smith's ct., fr. 515 Marriott
Smith's ct., fr. 618 S. Juniper
Smith's ct., f. 527 Lombard
Smith's pl., 928 N. 6th
Snyder, N. & S. 2100 S.
Snyder's al., E. fr. Fisher
Snyder's av., fr. 219 N. 23d
Snyder's ct., fr. 1218 Pearl
Snyder's ct., fr. 1300 Rye
Sober's al., fr. 415 Walnut
Sollady ct., fr. 415 Ann
Some set, E. & W. '830 N.
Somerset, fr. 4117 Mary
Somerville, E. & W. 5.00 N.
Somerville, fr. 2732 N. 12th
Sonora, fr. 1019 Morgan
Sophia, N. fr. Otter, b. l. 2d
Sorrel, E. fr. 10th, bel. Pi e
Souder, W. fr. F thergill
South, E. & W. 600 S.
S. Delaney pl., 2043 Lombard
S. Marshall, fr. 1122 S. 13th
Southampton pl., fr. Levant
Sower's ct, fr. 1420 Mifflin
Spafford, fr. 624 Alaska
Spangler, N. fr. Wrekin
Spark, N. fr. Bokius, (Bdg.)
Speilberger's ct., 1529 Hancock
Spencer pl., E. fr. Lybrand
Spencer's ct., fr. 2028 Lombard
Spooner's av., fr. 1130 St. John
Sprague, fr. Mill, (Gtn.)
Springer, N. fr. Gtn. av., (Gtn.)
Springfield av., S. W. fr. Baltimore av.
Spring, fr. 228 N. 16th
Spring, N. fr. Waln, (Fkd.)
Spring, fr. Manyunk av. (Myk)
Spring al., S. fr. Gtn. av. (Gtn.)
Springer's ct., fr. 120 Christian
Springett, fr. 630 N. 20th
Spring Garden, fr. 538 N. 6th
Spring Mill ct., fr. 43 N. 24th
Spruce, E & W. 300 S.
Square, W. fr. Rye,
Starr, S. McKean, ab. 8th
Stamper, W. fr. 422 S. 2d
Stanley, fr. 730 S. 3d
Stanton av., N. fr. Gtn. av. (Gtn)
Station, fr. Cottage, (Myk.)
Stanton pl., fr. 1624 N. 2d
Stapleton, S. fr. Carter
Starr al., S. fr. Race, ab. 5th
State, W. fr. 15th ab. Race
State, 3921 Market
Steadman, fr. 214 Quince
Steam Mill al., fr. 221 Willow
Stearley's ct., fr. Hermitage
Steck's ct., fr. 931 Rachel
Steel's ct., fr. 410 Bainbridge
Steiman ct., fr. 1419 Randolph
Steiner, S. fr. Melon, ab. 9th
Steinmetz pl., Market, ab. 34th
Steinrock, S. fr. Oxford, ab. 2d
Stella av., fr. 2924 Frankford av
Sterner fr. 2729 N. Front
Sterling, fr. 1629 Fitzwater
Stevenson's ct., fr. 9 9 S. 5th
Steward, N. fr. Manilla
Stewart, W. fr. 21st ab. Master
Stewart's ct., fr. 618 South
Stewa t's ct., fr. 14 Bainbridge
Stiles, fr. 1220 N. 11th
Stiles, N. fr. Ashland, (Fkd.)
Stiles, N. fr. Ashland, (Fkd.)
Stillman, S. fr. Oxford, ab. 25th
Stocker, S. fr. Carpenter, ab. 18th
Stockton, S. fr. Kemble, ab. 30th
Stock Exchange pl., fr. 132 S. 3d
Stockel, fr. 2021 Somerset
Stokes ct., fr. 245 Chester
Stone, fr. 421 S. 15th
Story, W. fr. 32d, ab. Haverford
Stoys, fr. 116 Beach
Stouten, N. fr. Hart's la.
Stranahan's ct., fr. 724 Bainbridge
Strangford pl., fr. 215 Christian
Stratford pl., fr. Rose al.
Stratton pl., fr. 131 Poplar
Stratton's ct., fr. 1421 Hancock
St. David's, N. fr. Race, ab. 23d
St. James' pl., fr. 22, ab. Spruce

St. John s pl., fr. 417 St. John
St. John, N. fr. Vine, ab. 2d
St. John's ct., fr. 723 St. John
St. Joseph's av., fr. 24 S. 17th
St. Mark's pl., fr. 4220 Walnut
St. Mary, fr. 528 S. 6th
St. Omar's pl., fr. 1726 Lombard
St. Paul's av., fr. 721 S. 7th
St. Stephen's pl., fr. 929 Chant
Strauss' ct., fr. 920 S. 6th
Strawberry, fr. 212 Market
Stretch, fr. 2124 Dickerson
Streper's ct., W. fr. 1029 Charlotte
Struthers, fr. 12th, ab. Race
Suffolk, fr. 1030 S. 8th
Sullivan, fr. Washington, (Gtn.)
Summer, fr. 15th, ab. Race
Summerfield pl, fr. 321 Green
Summit, fr. Gtn. av., (Gtu.)
Sun ct., fr. Ogden, ab. 9th
Surrey pl., 1009 St. John
Susanna, fr. 2417 Moyer
Susquebanna av., E. & W. 2200 N
Sussex, fr. 1123 Graff
Sutnerland, fr. 126 Queen
Sutter's ct., fr. 212 Carpenter
Sutton, fr. 5th, ab Master
Sutton's ct., fr. 1226 Beach
Swain, fr. 722 N. 25th
Swain's ct., fr. 227 Christian
Swanson, fr. 14 South
Swanson ct., fr. 842 Swanson
Swarthmore pl., fr. 229 N. 2d
Swartz, S. fr. Concord, ab. 2d
Sycamore, fr. Mill, (Gtn.)
Sycamore, fr. 1329 Spruce
Sydenham, fr. Master, ab. 15th
Sylvan, fr. 38th, bel. Poplar
Sylvester, fr. 16 6 S. 5th
**Tackawana**, fr. Church (Fkd)
Tacony, fr. Frankford, (Fkd.)
Tagert, fr. Norris, ab. Gaul
Tahasa, fr. 9th, ab. York
Talmage, fr. 221 Willow
Tamarind, fr. 117 Green
Tams ct., fr. 528 Barnwell
Tan la., fr. Church, (Fkd.)
Taney, fr. Perot, ab. 26th
Tanner, fr. McIlwain, ab. 4th
Tappen pl., fr. 719 Green
Tariff pl., fr. 428 N. 10th
Tasker, E. & W., 1600 S.
Tatlow, fr. 430 S. 18th
Taylor. W. fr. 8th, ab. Tasker
Taylor, N. fr. Hare, ab. 24th
Taylor, fr. Amber, ab. York
Taylor, E. fr. Biddle
Taylor's ct., fr. 719 S. 3d
Taylor's ct., fr. 2210 Naudain
Temple, fr. 1028 S. 12th
Ten-feet al., fr. 620 Barclay
Tenor pl., fr. 418 S. 4th
Test av., fr. Dunton

Thames, fr. 2728 Tulip
Thomas, S. fr. Ash, (Bdg)
Thomas, N. fr. Tacony, (Fkd.)
Thomas ct., fr. 1018 Hamilton
Thomazine, W. fr. Hollinger
Thompson, E. & W. 1300 N.
Thompson pl., fr. 122 Race
Thorn's ct., fr. 1121 Melon
Thouron, fr. Diamond, ab. 5th
Thurlow. fr. 814 S. 11th
Tibben, fr. Fountain, (Myk.)
Tiernan, S. fr. 1408 Ellsworth
Tilden, fr. 540 Chatham
Tilton, fr. 721 E. Cumberland
Tiller's ct., fr. 219 Vaughn
Time's ct., fr. 929 Rodman
Time's pl., fr. 521 Chatham
Timothy, fr. 219 Madison
Tinden's ct., fr. 211 Dean
Tinnal, fr. 1331 Locust
Tioga, E. & W. 3500 N.
Tisdale pl., fr. 228 Christian
Titan, W. fr. 16th, ab. Wharton
Titlow, S. fr. Tioga, ab. Tilton
Toland, E. fr. 20th, ab. Cherry
Tomlin ct., 937 Rachel
Ton al., fr. 120 S. Delaware av.
Torin, S. fr. Tioga, 620 E.
Toronto, E. fr. Melvale
Torpin, N. Clearfield, ab. Bath
Torr, W. fr. 9th, ab. Vine
Torr ct., N. fr. Torr, ab. 9th
Tottenham pl., fr. 819 Carpenter
Tower, fr. 126 N. 20.h
Tower, N. fr. Cedar, (Mvk.)
Townsend, fr. 2028 Cedar
Tood, N. fr. Oxford, bel. Front
Traquair's ct., fr. 19 N. 10th
Treaty av., fr. 930 N. 7th
Treft's ct., fr. 1329 Hancock
Tremont pl., fr. 1232 Pearl
Tremont pl., fr, Aspen, ab. 40th
Trent pl., fr. Weaver
Trenton av., fr, 31 E. Montg'y av
Trenton av., N. fr. Gay, (Myk.)
Trinity pl., fr. 122 Catharine
Trinity pl., fr. 314 S. 22d
Troller, fr. 1624 S. Front
Trotters, fr, 41 Norris
Trotters al., fr. 20 S. 2d
Trout, W. fr. Barrow
Truxton, S. fr. Budd
Tryon, W. fr. 21st, ab. South
Tucker, S. fr. Tacony cr., (Bdg)
Tucker, fr. 2638 Cedar
Tudor, N. fr. Tasker, ab. 7th
Tudor's ct., fr. 617 Marriott
Tulip, N. fr. Harrison
Tulpehocken. fr. Pulaski (Gtn.)
Turner, fr. 521 Ontario
Turner, W. fr. 19th, ab. Oxford
Turner's ct., fr. 112 Ohio
Turner's ct., fr. 720 Lombard

Tuscalum, fr. 2720 C.
Twaddell's ct,, fr. 1817 Barker
Twelve-foot al., fr. Metcalf
Tyler, S. fr. Master, ab. 9th
Tyler, W. fr. Faulkner
Tyson, fr. 2230 N. 6th, ab. 19th
**Uber,** S. fr. Norris
Uffenheimer's av., fr. 221 Poplar
Ulrick, S. fr. Maria
Ulrich's row, fr. 1322 N. 2d
Unadilla, fr. 1128 Passyunk
Union, fr. 318 S. Front
Union av., W. fr. Gtn. av. (Gtn.)
Union, fr. 3931 Havorford
Unity, W. fr. Walnut, (Fkd.)
Upsal, fr. Wissahickon av. (Gtn)
Upshur av., fr. 327 New Market
Urbanna pl., fr. 12 N. 9th
Utica pl., W. fr. Fothergill
**Valeria,** W. fr. 814 N. 6th
Valley ct., E. fr. Eutaw
Van Buren pl., fr. 842 Holland pl
Vanilla, fr. 39th, ab. Oregon
Van Pelt, N. fr. Norris, ab. 21st
Van Blunk's ct., fr. 515 Marriott
Vandeveer, fr. 918 Locust
Vanhorn, fr. 1130 Hancock
Vasey, W. fr. 17th, ab. Pine
Vaughn, S. fr. Walnut, ab. 15th
Venango, E. & W. 3600 N
Vermont, fr. 928 N. 7th
Verner, fr. 2821 Christian
Vernon, fr. 820 N. 10th
Vicker's ct., fr. 1719 Barker
Victoria, fr. 3631 Richmond
Viddal's al., fr. 2d, ab. Walnut
Vienna, fr. 1834 Beach
Vincent, Buttonwood, ab. 2d
**Vincent,** fr. Adams, (Myk.)
Vinc, E. & W. 300 N
Vineyard, fr. 933 N. 24th
Virginia, fr. 3133 Amber
Viola, fr. 41st, ab. Girard av.
Vining pl., fr. 243 Catherine
Vinton, E. fr. 3d, bel. Moore
Virginia, fr. 728 N. 22d
Vista, fr. Locust, ab. 18th
Volkmar, fr. Palmer, ab. Wildey
**Wabash** fr. 30 N. Front
Wadsworth pl., fr. 718 Filbert
Wager, fr. W. 5th, ab. Poplar
Wagner ct., fr. 630 N. 7th
Wakefield, fr. Bringhurst, (Gtn.)
Wakeling, fr. Frankford, (Fkd.)
Walker's ct., fr. 614 Willow
Wall, fr. 819 S. 7th
Walker, fr. Lehigh av. ab. Gaul
Walker, fr. Frankford, (Fkd.)
Wallace, W. fr. 7th, ab. Green
Waln, W. fr. 8th, bel. Reed
Waln, fr. Unity, (Fkd.)
Walnut, E. & W. 200 S
**Walnut la.,** W. fr. Gtn. av. (Gtn.)
**Walnut pl.,** S. fr. Walnut, ab. 3d

Walnut pl., fr. 3522 Sansom
Walter, fr. 1228 N. 15th
Walton ct., fr. 1622 Richard
Walton ct., fr. 529 Chatham
Walton's ct., fr. 420 Lynd
Wamly pl., fr. 1724 N. 2d
Ward, S. fr. Carpenter, ab. 18th
Ward's ct., fr. 23 Parham
Warder, S. fr. Berks, bel. Front
Warminster pl., fr. 1534 Cadwalader
Warner's ct., fr. 315 Bainbridge
Warner's ct., fr. 729 Carpenter
Warnock, N. fr. Poplar, ab. 10th
Warren, W. fr. 33d, ab. Market
Warthman's ct., fr. 2229 Tulip
Washington, N. fr. Main, (Myk.)
Washington, S. fr. Adams, (Fkd)
Washington av., E. & W. 1100 S
Washington av., (Fkd.)
Washington av., (Gtn.)
Washington ct. fr. 641 Lombard
Washington sq., fr. 634 S. 6th
Waterloo, fr. 137 Jefferson
Watkins, W. fr. 4th ab. Moore
Watt, fr. 420 S. 20th
Water, N. fr. 15 South
Water, S. fr. Bridge, (Bdg.)
Water la., fr. Gtn. av., (Gtn.)
Watts, fr. 1322 McKean
Waverly, fr. 428 S. 17th
Wayne, S. fr. Wallace, ab. 9th
Wayne av., fr. Roberts av., (Gtn.)
Weaver ct., E. fr. 1529 Gtn. av.
Webb, S. fr. Fitzwater, ab. 16th
Webb ct., fr. 224 Christian
Webster, fr. 826 S. 17th
Webster Ter., fr. Green la., (Myk)
Webster ct., fr. 718 Passyunk av
Weccacoe, N. fr. Queen, ab. 4th
Week's ct., fr. 932 Rachel
Weikel, N. fr. Ann, ab. Tulip
Welch, S. fr. Spruce, ab. 26th
Well's ct., fr. 1221 Randolph
Wellington pl. fr. 131 Dana
Wellington pl., fr. 3.25 Cedar
Welsh, fr. 520 S. 25th
Wenderly's ct., fr. 1013 N. 4th
West, S. fr. Parrish, ab. 19th
West, fr. 2329 Walnut
West, fr. 3212 Frankford av.
W. Delancy pl., fr. 324 S. 20th
Western av., fr. 220 15th
Westford av., fr 808 Noble
W. Logan, N. fr. Morris, (Gtn.)
Westminster av., fr. 800 N. 32d
Westmore pl., fr. 519 N. 2d
Westmoreland, E. & W. 3 0 N.
W. Shippen pl., fr. 821 Bainbridge
Wetherill, S. fr. 1416 Pine
Weyand's pl., E. fr. Elk
Wharf, fr Frankford cr., (Fkd.)
Wharton, E. & W. 1.5) S.

Wheat, W. fr. Crease
Wheat, N. fr. Cherry, ab. 10th
Wheat, S. fr. Marion, bel. 2d
Wheatsheaf la., fr. 3822 N. Delaware av.
Wheelock's pl., fr. 1319 Potts
Whelan's ct., fr. 1506 South
Whilden's row, E. fr. Rye
Whimple, fr. 918 Swanson
White, fr. 1612 Tulip
White, W. fr. 712 Lloyd
Whitebread pl., fr. 118 Christian
Whitecar's row, fr. 224 N. 5th
Whitehall, fr. 432 N. 12th
Whitehead's ct., fr. 728 S. 4th
Whiteman's ct., fr. 1240 Amber
White's ct., fr. 1328 Alaska
White's ct., fr. 925 N. 19th
White's Retreat, fr. 1029 N. 4th
Whitney, fr. 1134 S. 8th
Whyte's pl., fr. 1230 South
Wilcox, fr. 522 N. 19th
Wilcox, fr. 536 N. 36th
Wilder, W. fr. 4th, bel. Reed
Wildey, N. fr. 1121 Fkd. av.
Wile's ct., fr. 1319 Wallace
Wiley's ct., fr. 228 N. 11th
Willard, fr. 3221 Jasper
William, fr. 28 0 N. Del. av.
William, fr. 240 S. 20th
William, N. fr. Ash, (Bdg.)
William's al., fr. Metcalf, ab. 5th
William's ct., fr. 917 Callowhill
William's ct., fr. E. Montgomery
Williamson's ct., fr. 913 Cherry
Williamson's ct, 1124 Swanson
Willington, fr. 1625 Master
Willow, N. fr. Meadow, (Fkd.)
Willow la., E. fr. Haines, (Gtn.)
Willow, fr. 418 N. Delaware av.
Wilmer, E. fr. 2d, ab. Vine
Wilmer's al., 4th, ab. Vine
Wilson, fr. 324 Otsego
Wilson, E. fr. Metcalf
Wilson, S. fr. York, ab. Gaul
Wilson, E. fr. Haines, (Gtn.)
Wilson's ct., fr. 9 Poplar
Winchester ct., 1815 Alaska
Winchester pl., fr. 926 Otsego
Winfield, fr. 914 S. Front
Winfield pl., E fr. 8th, ab. Arch
Wingohocking, E. & W. 4500 N.
Winner pl., fr. 24 South
Winona, N. fr. Pulaski, (Gtn.)
Winslow, W. fr. 12th, ab. Race
Winter, W. fr. 16th ab. Race
Winter's ct., S. fr. Monterey
Winton, W. fr. 5th, ab. Jackson
Wirth's ct., fr. 829 N. 5th
Wirt pl., fr. 536 Linden
Wiss thickon av., (Gtn.)
Wiser, E. fr. Almond, (Bdg.)
Wishart's ct., fr. 104 Beach
Wishner, fr. 10th, bel. McK an

Wister, W. fr. 10th, bel. Green
Wister, N. fr. Gtn. av., (Gtn.)
Wister pl., 10tb ab. Green
Wisteria, E. & W. 5300 N.
Witte, N. fr. Clearfield, ab Cedar
Witzel's ct., fr. 1321 N. 25th
Wolff, E. & W. 2300 S.
Woelper's ct., E. fr. 23d, ab. Arch
Wolbert, N. fr. Taylor
Wolf's ct., S. fr. German ab. 3d
Wolf's ct., fr. 107 Lombard
Wolf's ct., E. fr. Hope, ab Stiles
Womroth pl., fr. 227 Monroe
Wonderly pl., fr. 145 Otter
Wood, W. fr. 2d ab. Vine
Wood, E. fr. Green la., (Myk.)
Wood, fr. Gtn. av. (Gtn.)
Woodbine, fr. Federal, ab. 6th
Woodbine av., S. fr. Chew, (Gtn.)
Woodland Ter., W. fr. Woodland av. ab. 38th
Woodland av., fr. 3260 Market
Woodland, fr. 330 S. 39th
Woodville pl., fr. St. Joseph's av
Wood's ct., W. fr. Greenhill
Woodstock, fr. 2020 Columbi av.
Woodworth av., fr. 14 Christian
Worrell, E.fr. Frankford, (rkd.)
Worth, W. fr. 3d, ab. Tasker
Worth, N. fr. Oxford, (Fkd.)
Wrekin, fr. 2622 Cedar
Wright, W. fr. 1530 N. 21st
Wright, W. fr. 32d ab. Market
Wyalusing, fr. 830 N. 42d
Wyandotte, fr. Wister, (Gtn.)
Wyatt, E. fr. Sidmouth
Wykoff, fr. 3228 Race
Wylie, fr. 1648 Ridge av.
Wynkoop, fr. 13th, ab. Spruce
Wyoming, fr. Ann, ab. Cedar
Wyoming, N. fr. 1515 Fitzwater
Wyoming av., fr. Gtn. av., (Gtn.)
Wyoming, E. & W., 4800 N.
Wyoming, W. fr. 2d, ab. Reed
Wyoming, fr. Market, ab. 40th
**Yale**, S. fr. Mifflin, ab. 20th
Yardley, fr. Master, ab. 20th
Yeager's ct., fr. 706 St. Mary
Yhost, S. fr. Catherine, ab. 5th
Yhost pl., fr. 625 Catherine
York, E. & W. 2400 N.
York av., N. fr. 4th ab. Vine
York pl., E. fr. 5th, ab Brown
Young, fr. Church, (Bdg.)
Young's al., fr. 426 New Market
Young's al., fr. Pegg, bel. 2d
Young's ct., fr. 233 Bainbridge
Young's ct., fr. 422 Carpenter
**Zanoni**, fr. 530 N. 24th
Zechariah ct., S. fr. Gothic
Zeig er ct., fr. Melvale
Zenobia, W.fr. 11th, bel. Walnut
Zephyr av. fr 7 0 S. 8th
Zimmerman, fr. 6th, ab. Oxford

# SOOY'S
# DINING SALOON
## No. 525 Chestnut Street.

To the resident it is unnecessary to say anything of this popular establishment, it having been in existence now nearly fifty years, during all of which time it has maintained a prominent position and an enviable reputation. The stranger visiting the city should know that for **a substantial meal of the best the market affords, served in the best style in a quiet manner, at moderate prices. IT IS UNEXCELLED, if equaled, by any in the country. The location is convenient,** being directly opposite Independence Hall and in the immediate vicinity of the prominent business houses, courts, banks, etc.

**ONE CALL WILL CONVINCE.**

☞ Elegantly fitted up rooms for the accommodation of ladies.

---

# RUFUS ADAMS,
# ELOCUTIONIST
## No. 1006 Chestnut Street,

‡ DELINEATOR OF SHAKESPEARE AND OTHER POETS. ‡

---

## CARPET PAPERS, BEST IN THE WORLD.
# J. C. DITMAN & CO.,
### SIXTH AND CHESTNUT STS.,
## The Largest Paper House in America!

*The Greatest Stock and Largest Variety.*
*Estimates Given on Large Contracts.*

# OLD BOOKS
— BOUGHT & SOLD. —

**PICKWICK & CO.**
1429 MARKET ST.
— PHILADELPHIA. —

## Rare and Curious Books on Hand and Furnished.

**ORDERS SOLICITED.**

---

**Harper's Hair Dye.** Guaranteed under a forfeiture of $50 to contain no lead or sulphur. Harmless, natural, indetectable, and does not fade or wash out; gives uniform brown or black to suit the complexion; no one would be without it after once using it; no ridiculous tints; always takes; never fails; no trouble to apply; sold at 50 cents a box; superior to any other, though costing twice as much; it is not a wash or pretended regenerator or restorer, yet it certainly benefits the hair, without injuring the health or skin. Ask your druggist, perfumer or hairdresser for it.

NOTE.—It is the only article that can always be relied upon to give a natural uniform color, no matter how often applied.

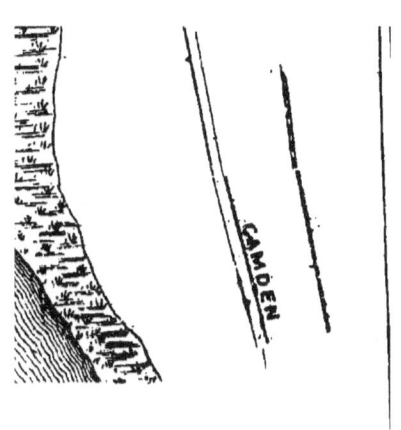

# eirce College of Business,

## NEW RECORD BUILDING,
## 919 CHESTNUT STREET,
### PHILADELPHIA.

MAS MAY PEIRCE, M.A.,      REV. JOHN THOMPSON,
EXPERT ACCOUNTANT), PRINCIPAL.      DEAN.

---

College teaching technical knowledge qualifying for business
gements. Possessing all the facilities and having established
haracter, it is now prepared to give its classes full instruction
ommercial and general business vocations.

---

**WHILE,** Agent for Holland's Gold Pens and New Slide Business Pencil. Mac- ınd Stylographic Pens. № 335 CHESTNUT Street.

Call or send for prices.

**PENS REPAIRED**

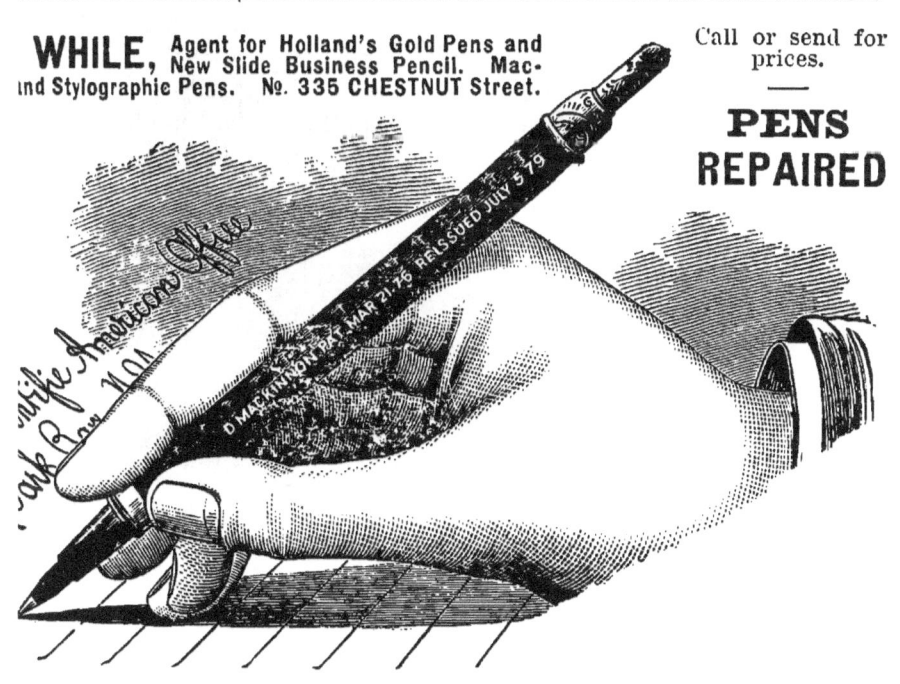

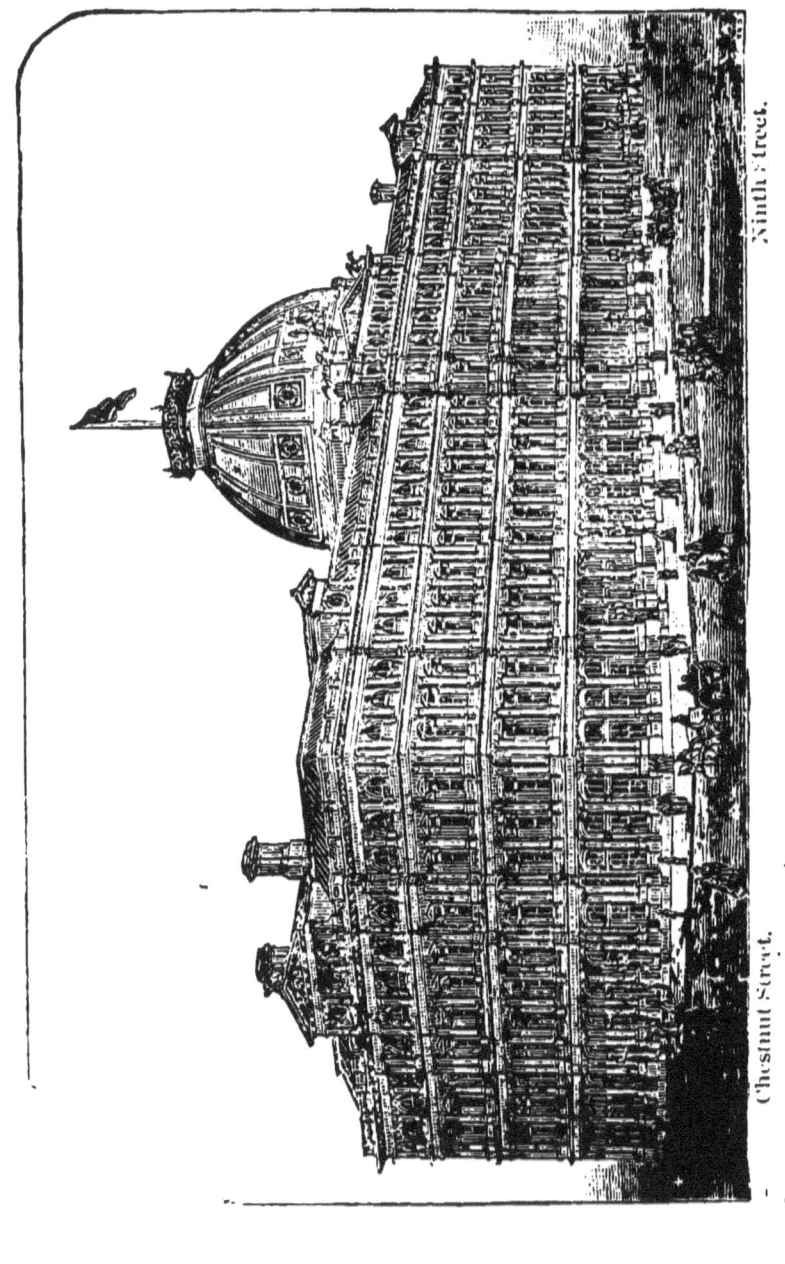

NEW POST-OFFICE.

www.ingramcontent.com/pod-product-compliance
Lightning Source LLC
Chambersburg PA
CBHW020154170426
43199CB00010B/1031